WAHIDA CLARK DISTRIBUTION

THE MAN WITH THE SOLUTION:

From Addiction to Recovery to Power

Henry Duane Muhammad (Hamilton),
MS, LCADC, ICADC, CAMF

W. Clark Distribution & Media Corp.

Wahida Clark Distribution
60 Evergreen Place
Suite 904A
East Orange, New Jersey 07018
1-866-910-6920
www.wclarkdistribution.com
www.wclarkpublishing.com

Copyright 2019 © by Henry Duane Muhammad (Hamilton)

All rights reserved. This book, or parts thereof, may not be reproduced in any form without permission.

Library of Congress Cataloging-In-Publication Data:
Henry Duane Muhammad (Hamilton)
The Man with The Solution: From Addiction to Recovery to Power
ISBN 13-digit 9781947732391
ISBN 10-digit 9781947732
LCCN: 2019943683

1. Mental Health- 2. Behavioral Health 3. Substance Abuse- 4. Addictions- 5. Incarceration 6. War on Drugs- 7. Opioid Epidemic

Creative direction & layout by Art Supplied Gfx
www.artdiggs.com

Printed in USA

TABLE OF CONTENTS

INTRODUCTION 1

    Who is Dr. Muhammad? 1

    What message does Mr. Muhammad want to get across to the audience? 2

    What is a mental health disorder? 4

    Why is the Mental Health Field and the Addictions Field Divided? 7

    Mental Illness Data 8

    2010 Data for New Jersey 10

    How did you get into the field of behavioral healthcare and substance use services? 11

    What is a substance use disorder? 19

    Can you give more information on your substance use and mental health problems? 22

    What is 'Rock Bottom'? 26

What was your experience with heroin? 28

Does Behavioral Healthcare really work? 31

The difference between Use, Abuse and Dependence 38

Are people who become dependent on drugs or alcohol weak or evil people? 40

Is substance use and mental illness hereditary? 43

Does the government have something to do with the problem of substance use disorder? 46

What are the signs and symptoms of substance and/or alcohol use disorder? 51

How can substance use disorder be prevented? 54

Is there such a thing as social substance use? 58

Does substance use affect your creativity and ability to master certain skills? 60

What is it like to perform before thousands of people sober? 63

Do artists need drugs and/or alcohol to perform or create material? 67

What is an example of being a functioning drug addict? 70

What approach do you take when dealing with mental disorder or substance use dependence? 74

At what point does substance use become dependence? 76

What is Post Incarceration Syndrome (PICS)? How does it relate to Post Traumatic Stress Disorder (PTSD)? 78

Medical Marijuana 83

What is medical marijuana? 84

What is medical marijuana used for? 85

How does it help? 86

How can medical marijuana help with seizure disorders? 87

Which states allow medical marijuana? 87

How do you get medical marijuana? 89

How do you take it? 89

Has the FDA approved medical marijuana? 90

What are the side effects of medical marijuana? ... 90

Slideshow: Medical Marijuana 91

How It Works in Your Body 93

Are There Risks? 93

What Are FDA-Approved Versions of Medical Marijuana? 95

Are There Any Laws in Conflict Regarding Medical Marijuana? 96

Do People Become Addicted? 97

Why Don't We Know More? 98

Is Cannabis an Opioid Alternative? 99

References 101

INTRODUCTION

Who is Dr. Muhammad?

Henry Duane Muhammad (Hamilton), MS, LCADC, ICADC, CAMF, Doctoral Candidate, Founder and CEO of Prodigal Sons and Daughters Behavioral HealthCare Services

Mr. Muhammad (Hamilton) is a New Jersey Licensed Clinical Alcohol and Drug Counselor with a master's degree in counseling psychology. He is a doctoral candidate, internationally certified in the field of addiction counseling and a certified anger management facilitator. He has worked in the field of mental health and addiction counseling for thirty-three years and has lectured all over the country. He is an Advocate Leader for the National Council of Alcohol and Drug Dependence of New Jersey and has testified before State legislatures, department heads and stakeholders concerning the stigma of mental health and substance use disorder and the importance of funding. He was also commissioned by the Essex County Executive to serve on the Local Advisory Committee for Alcohol and Drug Abuse and has served three terms. Mr. Muhammad is also an accomplished concert performer, recording artist and manages a classic soul group known as the Silver

Stars.

Mr. Muhammad's passion for his work grows out of his own rehabilitation from alcohol, drug use disorder, mental illness, criminal involvement and homelessness. His journey has gone from hopelessness to becoming the founder and chief executive officer of a New Jersey State License comprehensive outpatient ambulatory healthcare facility. The facility provides treatment for substance use, mental illness, co-occurring disorders, primary medical services and recovery supports, i.e., vocational and academic enrichment, job placement and community service. In collaboration with the Prodigal Sons and Daughters Prisoner Re-entry Initiative and the New Jersey Food Bank, the behavioral healthcare initiative opened a Community Resource Center and Gratuitous Living Program which provides recovery support in the way of transitional housing and a food pantry to service the basic needs of the consumers, their families, the community and the worried well.

What message does Mr. Muhammad want to get across to the audience?

The message most prominent in this work is that Mr. Muhammad has created a treatment model that works! It is genuine, culturally sensitive, empathic, and evidenced based with proven practice!

The author credits his Higher Power as the source and

guiding light of his work. He attributes his universal perspective, which may not necessarily agree in concept with the ever-changing ideals of the mainstream treatment perspectives, to his parents and ancestral lineage. By mainstream, he's referring to The Substance Abuse and Mental Health Services Administration (SAMHSA), the American Society of Addiction Medicine (ASAM) and the National Institute of Drug Abuse (NIDA). In fact, the author suggests that just as the disease of mental illness and addiction has many causative factors that are as diverse as the people who suffer with these illnesses, i.e., culture, gender, race, creed, class, religion, etc., the approach to treatment must be just as diverse.

He doesn't speak in contravention to these institutions and deeply appreciates the research, findings, literature, colleges and universities that have been produced under their auspices. However, as a healthcare practitioner, and one who has experienced chronic addiction, mental illness, criminal involvement and homelessness, with over thirty years in full sustained remission and treating this population, he has developed a model that is foolproof! His model integrates his personal experience and most of the evidenced-base practices into a proven practice system with universal methodologies that have worked for thousands of the consumers he has worked with throughout his career.

The author submits that the cornerstone of this treatment paradigm is empathy. "Dr., heal thyself first!" As such he has established an ambulatory care facility that is wholistic and comprehensive in scope; with that, it deals with every aspect of the person; mentally, physically and spiritually(emotionally) and not necessarily in that order. The system is designed to meet the person where they are and then, step by step, give them the power to manage and change their condition. Prodigal Sons And Daughters Behavioral HealthCare Services provides behavioral healthcare services for mental health, substance use and co-occurring disorders from prevention/intervention, treatment, housing, vocational training, entrepreneurial development, financial literacy, job coaching and placement. He has also entered into collaborations with community colleges and universities and set up an internship initiative that provides students with the opportunity to gain practical experience and develop the clinical skills necessary to work in the field of behavioral healthcare.

What is a mental health disorder?

Mental illness refers to a wide range of mental health conditions—disorders that affect your mood, thinking and behavior. Examples of mental illness include depression, anxiety disorders, schizophrenia, eating disorders and addictive behaviors.

According to the American Psychiatric Association, mental illnesses are health conditions involving changes in emotion, thinking or behavior (or a combination of these). Mental illnesses are associated with distress and/or problems functioning in social, work or family activities.

Mental illness is common and it's treatable. The vast majority of individuals with mental illnesses continue to function in their daily lives. According to Mental Health America, a mental illness is a disease that causes mild to severe disturbances in thought and/or behavior, resulting in an inability to cope with life's ordinary demands and routines.

There are more than 200 classified forms of mental illness. Some of the more common disorders are depression, bipolar disorder, dementia, schizophrenia and anxiety disorders. Symptoms may include changes in mood, personality, personal habits and/or social withdrawal.

Mental health problems may be related to excessive stress due to a situation or a series of events. As with cancer, diabetes and heart disease, mental illnesses are often physical as well as emotional and psychological. Mental illnesses may be caused by a reaction to environmental stresses, genetic factors, biochemical imbalances or a combination of these. With proper care and treatment, many individuals learn to cope or recover from a mental illness or an emotional disorder.

The above three definitions in the first three paragraphs of this section come from three distinct sources and are, in my opinion, merely the tip of the iceberg as it relates to what a mental health disorder really is. I'm willing to suggest that not only is it a mood, thinking and behavioral abnormality, but it is an interruption in the natural order and functioning of any human being down to the core of their very existence. This causes an adverse reaction to the natural thought processes in the brain to the point of major dysfunction and distraction in the human dynamic. It is my belief that the basis of health and wellness begins with self-awareness or the knowledge of self. Also, we must understand that mental illness in one culture or civilization may be considered normal in another. I have treated individuals who were diagnosed by a licensed psychiatrist, social worker or whomever with mental illness according to *the Diagnostic Statistical Manual of Mental Disorders*. During my work with the individual, I found their survival skills and intelligence to far exceed some people who are considered learned and credentialed in this society.

It is also amazing to me how psychiatrists, social workers, professional and addiction counselors all use the same manual to diagnose; they are all cross-trained because of the reality of co-occurring or co-morbid concerns in mental health, yet there seems to be a turf war, if you will, when it comes to who can diagnose and treat persons with mental illness. The problem is that the human condition continues to depreciate because of this separation among so-called professional providers. One is often left to wonder, who's really sick?

Why is the Mental Health Field and the Addictions Field Divided?

In my humble opinion it is because of money, politics, misinformation and in some cases outright deceit. There are many professionals in both fields that are making tremendous strides in helping persons with mental illness and addiction manage and, in some cases, even reverse their illness using nontraditional protocols. Of course, these individuals are not supported by the Food and Drug Administration (FDA) which supports and backs up the traditional protocols. In most cases the traditional protocols treat the symptoms of the illness and not the root cause. This is scientifically known and well documented yet ignored by the healthcare conglomerate. There is much to be said on this subject; it can be made into book form itself but suffice it to say as it is said in *Uncle Yah Yah 21st Century Man of Wisdom*, "knowledge is not confined to any institution of learning". "Knowledge if a free man and it knows no bounds". Substance use disorder is relatively new as a 'specialty practice' requiring licensure because, in the not so distant past, individuals with substance use disorder: heroin, cocaine, crack, barbiturates, methamphetamine, hallucinogens, etc., where looked at as criminal, diabolical, evil and worthy of nothing but punishment. Alcohol use which became socially acceptable after prohibition has less stigma attached to it, though, according to most research it kills more people annually than all of the other psychoactive substances combined. Most mental health professionals, social workers, psychologists, psychoanalysts, etc., do not see the addictions professional as an equal contributor to the health and wellbeing of a consumer. However, there is a very thin line between the mental, emotional and behavioral condition of a person with substance use disorder and a person with mental illness. And though these professions use the same book to diagnose, there is territorial divide that says who can diagnose who, while those suffering with mental illness and substance use disorder die.

Mental Illness Data

- Serious mental illnesses costs America $193.2 billion in lost earnings per year.

Adolescents

According to the National Alliance On Mental Illness (NAMI), "Prevalence of Mental Illness."

- Approximately 21.4% of youth, aged 13-18, experience a severe mental disorder at some point during their life. For children aged 8-15, the estimate is 13.3%.

- 70% of youth in juvenile justice systems have at least one mental health condition, and at least 20% live with a serious mental illness.

Adults
- Approximately 1 in 5 adults in the U.S.—43.8 million, or 18.5%—experience mental illness in a given year.

- An estimated 26% of homeless adults staying in shelters, live with serious mental illness and an estimated 46% live with severe mental illness and/or substance use disorders.

- Individuals living with serious mental illnesses face an increased risk of having chronic medical conditions.17 adults in the U.S. living with serious mental illnesses die, on average, 25 years earlier than others, largely due to treatable medical conditions.

- Approximately 20% of state prisoners and 21% of local jail prisoners have "a recent history" of a mental health condition.

In a given year:

- Nearly one in five (19 percent) of U.S. adults experience some form of mental illness.

- One in 24 (4.1 percent) have a serious mental illness.

- One in 12 (8.5 percent) have a diagnosable substance use disorder

2010 Data for New Jersey

- Alcohol and drug addiction are the most serious health problems facing us today. Over 70% of the country believes addiction is a disease that should be treated as any other chronic disease.

- In the state of New Jersey, of more than 800,000 who have an alcohol or drug problem, only 7% are admitted for treatment due to limited capacity.

- Over 50,000 people who sought treatment in New Jersey were unable to access it due to limited capacity.

- The Alcohol Education, Rehabilitation, and Enforcement Fund that provides treatment money to counties, has not seen a rise since 1992. This causes counties to run out of money halfway through the year and leaves thousands of individuals without access to addiction treatment.

- 75% of those incarcerated have either substance use, mental health, and/or co-occurring disorders.

It is beyond doubt that addiction treatment saves taxpayer dollars. It will reduce budget costs to the state such as those incurred for healthcare, public safety, criminal justice, worker's compensation, welfare, child abuse and neglect, and improved employment.

Creating access to treatment saves lives, renews hopes, restores families, and heals illness. 11.4% or $3.7 billion of state budgets go to address the problems arising from alcohol and drug misuse, and only .3% goes to prevention treatment and research. For every dollar spent on substance abuse, 97cents is spent on the burden to public programs for untreated addiction, 2cents on treatment, 1cent on prevention, and 1cent on regulation compliance.

Tight government budgets and continued economic turmoil result in a strong temptation to cut social programs in order to maintain budget discipline. But not all budget cuts result in cost savings. Investing in effective addiction treatment now, will enable meaningful cost savings in the future, both short and long-term.

How did you get into the field of behavioral healthcare and substance use services?

It was in the fall of 1985, but I can remember it like it was yesterday. A friend of mine from the streets, meaning he was not a close personal friend, but a colleague of the streets, and I were sitting on a park bench across the street from Newark's City Hall. We were drinking Boone's Farms Apple Wine and we must've been on our second or third fifth! Wasn't nothing like Boone's Farm in those days when it came to drink! Anyway, we were having our usual afternoon, getting high and talking bad about the officials across the street in city hall. We talked about how they didn't know what they were doing, and how we should be in charge, because if we were over there running things, life would be much better for the community and residents of Newark.

Somewhere during this discourse of intellectual drunkenness, out of nowhere he informed me that to get the maximum amount of money from welfare (which happened to be my lot at that time) all you had to do was go into rehab! Of course, both of us were on welfare and doing bad, but I don't know why the brother said this, and I don't know why I remembered it when the time presented itself.

At the time, the welfare income was $130.00 a month; that was if you were an independent. If you lived with someone (parent, family member, significant other, etc.) which is considered support, you got less. Lo and behold, about three weeks later my welfare check was decreased to $65.00. When I went to the welfare office to inquire about this cut in pay, they said that I was living with my parents. That was very strange to me because I'd been homeless and living on the streets for about a year.

The disease of addiction is insidious, cunning, and baffling. I will be referring to these terms throughout the book because they described the subtle nature of the illness. The disease is insidious because the thought processes are deceptive and can often be sinister behavior. Cunning because it requires crafty articulation to obtain the substance and to try to hide the fact that you are under its influence. Baffling because of the mystery of addiction, especially before a person becomes aware that it is a brain disease. What is normal becomes abnormal and what is abnormal becomes normal.

Now back to the story, I lived wherever I could find a place. I became acquainted with drug dealers, pimps, players, prostitutes and hustlers from New York to Philadelphia. I slept in crack houses, shooting galleries, motels, brothels, county jails, park benches; wherever. I can remember living with a prostitute in her families' home, and she would leave me there for days in her room while she was in the streets handling her affairs. I can also remember riding with her family to New York and getting busted on the way back home with drugs in the car. We all went to jail that night, her included.

However, when welfare decreased my check to $65.00, I was livid! I was already militant in my perspective towards the United States government, so this just fed my psyche regarding the injustices and inequities of black people in America. Suddenly, the idea "you can get more money from welfare if you go to rehab" hit my mind like a ton of bricks! I was ready too; I mean I was sick and tired of being sick and tired. I was at rock bottom!

By this time, I had begun using heroin and cocaine intravenously. I also got caught up in the beginning of the 'urban crack', epidemic in the early 1980s. It started with a glass pipe and ended with smoking crack out of a screen filtered ink pen.

For me, going through active addiction was like going through major surgery with one's eyes open and little to no anesthesia. So, though my intentions for going to rehab were unrighteous to say the least, the experience reignited in me the catalyst that would change my life forever.

I decided to go to rehab and there was an outpatient program in downtown Newark called U-Can II (as I look back on this, what a perfect name for a rehab. Talk about subliminal seduction)! Now before I went in, of course I had to do 'one for the road' because I didn't know if they were going to send me away that night or what; this was my first encounter with the field of addictions treatment. So, I drank about a pint of wine and took a barbiturate (Tuinal) to prepare and when I went in the place I was as they say, 'toh up from the flo up!'

While there, I met one of the most pleasant older Black women that you could ever meet, she was to become my 'spiritual mother'. By this I mean the woman to birth me into my recovery and the field of addictions treatment. She offered me a seat in her office and began to question me as to why I was there. Being under the influence I was very guarded, obnoxious and in a serious state of denial. And it seemed the more negatively boisterous and difficult I tried to be, the calmer she became. I began demanding, "I want to go to rehab, I need to go to rehab!" She handed me an Alcoholics Anonymous meetings list and suggested that I try going to meetings first. I told her I didn't need to go to no meeting, I needed to go to rehab. In the back of my mind I was thinking about the increase in welfare dividends, I wasn't thinking about all this recovery stuff she was talking about. Anyway, it was late, and she gave me the meetings list and told me to come back tomorrow and she'd try to get me into a rehab program.

So, I left and as I was going to my favorite park bench where I was living at the time, I thought about how nice she was and some of the things she asked me and some of the things she said. One of my fondest memories of what she said to me was "God don't make no junk!" To make a long story short, I went back the next day and she introduced me to a dapper well-dressed Black Male counselor who is my sponsor to this day. He asked me a few questions, because in those days, that really tested your level of motivation for change. Though access to treatment was much more accessible, counselors still went all out to make sure that you really wanted to get help. He called a detox to make sure they had an opening, walked me to the bus stop and paid the driver and instructed the driver to not let me off until we reached the detox program. And this he did.

While in detox, I met another dapper Black Male counselor and he said, "drug addiction and alcoholism are diseases that negatively affect all aspects of your life: mentally, physically and spiritually (emotionally)!" After hearing those words, something like the telephone ringing went off in my head and I just couldn't get that thought out of my mind. I'd never heard that idea before; using drugs and alcohol is a sickness, not a curse, weakness or social norm, but a sickness? And it negatively effects every aspect of your life? Talk about identification. I became a model consumer. If the counselors said jump, I'd ask, how high? I forgot all about the increase in welfare! Seven days went by fast. I participated in psycho education and group therapy, individual counseling and urinalysis. They gave me vitamins, improved my diet and introduced me to Alcoholics and Narcotics Anonymous meetings for social support. Then they referred me to a twenty-one-day residential treatment facility called the 'RAFT' program to get more knowledge.

There I had a White Male counselor who wasn't dapper or anything like that but was very committed to the recovery process. He was a Burt Reynolds looking type. Anyway, I believe that the administrators of that program matched me with him because I was heavy into the civil rights movement, Black Power and Nationalism and I guess they wanted to see if I was wise enough and open minded enough to learn from anyone. Needless to say, it worked. I began to learn the various treatment concepts and modalities of recovery very fast. While in the program I returned to my original diet of fasting, eating one meal a day and physical exercise.

As my time there was ending, the counselor, who had learned that I had a great love for singing had me to sing a song to my peers. That was a very moving moment for me. Anyway, I completed the 21-day program and attended their outpatient program for about another 6 months while attending AA and NA meetings. Suddenly it came to me that I wanted to be a counselor, so I went back to college and started studying different schools of thought as it pertained to addictions treatment and recovery. I earned my degree, became certified and then became an oral evaluator for the certification board and on and on and on. So, I can truly say that I started at the bottom and have worked my way up and have helped countless others along the way.

Another memorable experience that lead me to this field was when I was younger, and my mother permitted me to have a sip of alcohol. She nor I had any idea that a seed was being planted. We didn't know it would evolve into approximately fifteen years, from that date, into a lifestyle of crime, abuse and dysfunction. We didn't know that it would lead to jail, welfare, homelessness and finally hospitalization (detox and residential treatment). But again, little did I know that this would be the process of learning that would lead to my present state of wellbeing. You know there's a saying, the darkest hour is just before the dawn! Another excellent edict is, the deeper the sorrow, the greater the joy! Also, no pain, no gain! This is known as cognitive reframing; when you can look at what's wrong and bring out of it that which is right. The industry uses cognitive reframing to help individuals look at life through different lenses. My concept is to reeducate the mind into thinking that all things in life serve a positive purpose once you know what your purpose in life is.

Only experience can make the above axioms true.

You can read it and talk about it, but to understand it you must go through it. When I found out that there was a course of study in colleges and universities that taught about mental illness and substance use disorder, I just had to check it out. Sure enough, I found my niche and my sole purpose in life. I discovered my voice is the key, because it articulates the sound that is the truth. And as it is said, the truth shall set you free!

What is a substance use disorder?

According to the American Psychiatric Association, addiction is a complex condition because it is a brain disease that is manifested by compulsive substance use despite harmful consequences. People with addiction (severe substance use disorder) have an intense focus on using a certain substance(s), such as alcohol or drugs, to the point that it takes over their life and they can no longer distinguish right from wrong, good from bad, life from death.

Now it is with this definition that I offer my most fervent concern as a practitioner. It appears that the Mental Health Association and most social workers are concerned with addiction counselors treating mentally ill consumers. But according to this definition by psychiatrists, addiction or substance use disorder is clearly a mental illness. It is a brain disease manifested by compulsive substance use despite harmful consequences. Even to the point where the disease takes over one's life, meaning their thoughts, mood, behavior, lifestyle, etc. Under the use of psychoactive substances an individual's entire being is transformed to the point of oblivion. The illness is such that one has to be treated on every human sphere of existence, mental, spiritual and physical, to get back to the normalcy called recovery or in more clinical terms, remission.

Substance use disorder (addiction) is described as insidious, cunning and baffling! There is no limit to which a person will go to satisfy their compulsion to use drugs, alcohol, food, people, etc. And it is further reported that there is no equal parallel to one addict helping another and thus you have the group therapy process, fellowship and peer counseling. Most professional practitioners, especially social workers and addiction counselors, who never suffered with the disease of addiction shun this concept. Because to say that there is no equal parallel to one addict helping another calls to questions their ability to empathize with those who suffer with the illness. However, it shouldn't; it's no different than a male gynecologist, who never experienced giving birth to a child, but understands what is required to deliver one.

I have learned over the years that the greatest hindrance to health and wellness for those who suffer with substance use disorder is healthcare bureaucracies in the form of Departments of Health and Human Services, that create division of mental health, addictions, family and children services. Also, insurance companies that make a fortune off prescription drugs that in many cases cause more harm than good.

I believe that making treatment more affordable, holistic in scope, residential care when necessary, and parity or equivalent compensation across the board as it pertains to insurance coverage is imperative if we truly want to increase positive outcomes. For example, Medicaid coverage needs to be on par with major insurance carriers so that the quality of care for addictions treatment can be the same as it is for any other chronic disease.

Substance use disorder is a chronic disease and it should be treated that way. We must do all that we can to do away with the negative stigma associated with use of drugs and alcohol and understanding that these individuals suffer with a chronic illness just like other's suffering from chronic illness.

Every day of my life, I have to monitor my illness, manage its symptoms and adhere to a recovery protocol to stay in remission. Because the illness, like cancer, is insidious and chronic, it requires a 24/7 watch, three hundred sixty-five days a year. I share this concept with my consumers to help them to understand that self-awareness and self-reflection is always of the utmost importance. In order to recover with substance use disorder, you must be mindful of your thoughts, attitude and behavior at all times because addiction impacts every aspect of one's being. A major concept in this regard is One Day at A Time! This can also be broken down to mean, one hour, one minute, one second; the idea is to always be in the present! The disease is always lurking to get you back in its grip. In fact, there is a term called 'PAW' (Post-Acute Withdrawal) which happens when a person enters into recovery and it could last for years. Addiction is like modern day slavery. It takes over your mind, body and soul. It is a chronic disease, but it can be arrested and managed, and persons can go on to live positive and productive lives in recovery. There are many paths that a person can take to recover but maintenance requires serious commitment. Spirituality, positive self-talk, meditation, jogging, walking, journaling, reading, healthy diet and positive social relationships are key elements in sustaining long term recovery.

Can you give more information on your substance use and mental health problems?

My mental illness is bipolar and mood disorder, and it went undiagnosed for years. By the grace and mercy of my Higher Power, whom I chose to call Allah, I have some semblance of stability in my life today without the use of psychotropic medication. I self-medicated my mental health issues with psychoactive substances, cannabis and all its derivatives, alcohol and all its derivatives, heroin and its derivatives and cocaine and its derivatives. Back in the day, they called this a 'garbage head', and in the treatment field they termed it poly substance use disorder! I am so thankful to be alive today, sober, in good health, strong and with a sound mind. I know myself, my God (Allah) and my purpose in life. Recovery to me means Resurrection! Addiction had me thinking that my greatest experience with euphoria from psychoactive substance use was when I overdosed on heroin. When the people I was with brought me back to consciousness, I felt like I was walking on water. I chased that high for the rest of my days only to learn that much like that first orgasm, there's only one to a customer. There will never be one like the first one.

I hope that my vulgarity is not being misinterpreted by the faint of heart, because persons with addiction disorder appreciate 'the real', and not some 'milk toast' jargon that accounts for nothing in the world in which they live. We're talking about the world of fantasy and make-believe, the world of the sly, the slick and the wicked! There is no limit to what I would do to reach euphoria. I would rob, cheat, steal, sell drugs, lie. There were no bounds. I couldn't be a father to my children and the drugs helped me escape only to realize that the problems kept getting worse. Being homeless for me became common place because I became too embarrassed to face my family members or true friends and I would find myself sleeping in some of the most bizarre places participating in some of the most high-risk behaviors.

One of the requirements for recovery is rigorous honesty! Since addiction, or substance use disorder, is a lifestyle of lies, cheating, stealing and self-deceit, it requires an equally opposite mindset to restore the normal functioning of the brain. Some researchers say that the brain will never regain normalcy or maximum potentiality, only near normal. I say, it depends on the tools you're working with. A remedy limited in scope can only produce limited results, but when you have a remedy that goes to the core, or what we call, the exact nature of the problem, then complete health and wellness is restored. Remember, addiction is a brain disease, in that, any psychoactive chemical used alters the normal chemical composition of the brain matter. So much so that natural mental, psychological and emotional growth of the human being stops. Physically he/she continues to age, but proper homeostatic development ceases, and there is an imbalance. Therefore, nothing can go right for a sustained period of time until effective treatment is administered.

"Physician heal thyself" is the base. The experience of active substance use and mental disorder for me was a transformative experience. In a book entitled *Uncle*

Yah Yah, 21st Century Man of Wisdom the author says, and I quote, "How could we know how distant far is, if it were not for those who go to the extreme?" I like the idea that no one size fits all, and that there is no such thing as cookie cutter treatment. I agree with that idea 100%. And this should be shared with consumers in treatment; empower them to find their own way. Nobody knows you like you know you, and it's the same for them. They don't know they have the keys, show it to them; be an example.

There is a lot of talk in the field of behavioral healthcare, mental health and addiction services about self-disclosure, appropriate self-disclosure, having nothing to disclose, etc., but the bottom line is, what is most effective for the consumer. I know one thing, if I'm in a foreign land it would surely be helpful to me to find somebody who at least, speaks my language. I have surmised that I will be in therapy for the rest of my life, because the life germ of the disease of mental illness and addiction is ever present in every human being in some shape, form or fashion. It must be managed, maintained and monitored with every fiber of our human existence. I think I said it earlier, what's normal for one culture may be abnormal to another. What's good to one may be bad to another, and for some there is no good or bad, normal or abnormal, it just is!

What is 'Rock Bottom'?

According to the Jellinek Curve of Addiction and Recovery, attached at the end of this section, 'Rock Bottom' is considered the point at which the obsession to use is purely out of control and unmanageable. The spiritual and moral compass is broken, and you enter a state wherein you "use to live and live to use". There is no limit that one will not go to access their substance of choice, or a derivative of that substance or a temporary substitution for it. The human being enters into a lawless state, and the brain is altered to the point wherein self-harm is already an accepted reality; and now, harm to others is in the crosshairs of the misery that is now seeking company. A symptom in this state is spiritual bankruptcy; rational decision making is exhausted, and the will is broken. The irony of this pathology is that it is the same regardless of race, class, creed or color. Once the disease of addiction gets to 'Rock Bottom', Dr. Jekyll will become Mr. Hyde! In fact, that transformation has already manifested itself in earlier stages, but this is the point of no return; it's either go to jail, the hospital, the cemetery or change. I went to jail and the hospital after a second overdose and another chance at life, I decided the cemetery could wait and I got sober.

Fear can be a great motivator, but I think love is superior. The key to change is driven by desire. One can have an idea to do something but if you don't have the will to do it, it won't happen. Research suggests that more than 75% of the incarcerated population are incarcerated as a direct result of psychoactive substance use disorder and most of them don't even know it! It's like gaining weight and getting sick but not acknowledging the fact that you're eating all types of starches, sweets, fast foods and other malnutrition food products and beverages five or six times a day every day. Dishonesty, cheating and stealing are the main symptoms of substance use disorder. As these symptoms progress without intervention or treatment so does the onset of the disease. So, if you don't know the warning signs or symptoms of the illness then the likelihood of becoming infected is heightened.

However strange it may appear to be, there is irony in being at the bottom. Because from the bottom, there is no place you can go but up! Uncle Yah Yah says, "the higher you aspire to the heights and lights, the deeper your roots go earthward and down into the depths of darkness." It reminds me of that story in the Bible where it says that in the beginning was darkness and yet out of that darkness God created light (the Sun)! Imagine that, out of darkness He created the Sun. So, if light can be created out of darkness, then it is possible to get good out of evil, right out of wrong and wellness out of sickness. And the impetus for this is desire. It is desire, not the necessity for treatment that helps the person become whole again. I try to inject the desire that I've garnered over the years, as a result of my experience and learning, into every consumer that I treat, and it works.

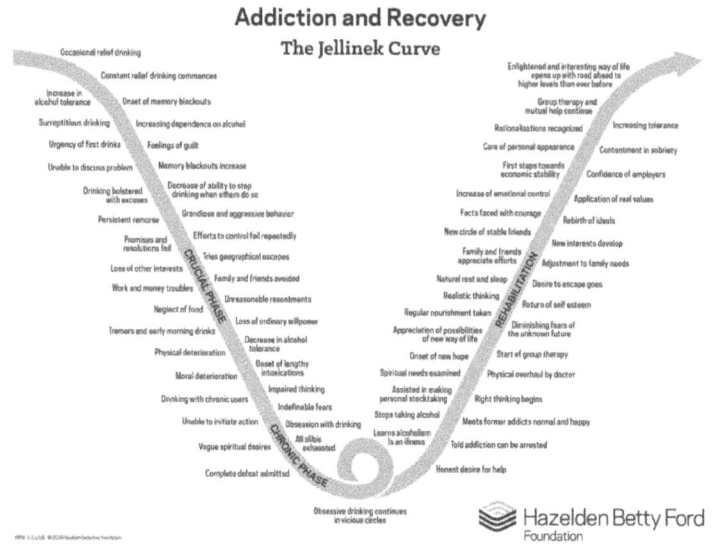

What was your experience with heroin?

I used heroin for approximately eight years. I started out inhaling, and it progressed to intravenous use almost immediately. It was immensely extraordinary. As I look back on it, I was 'speed ballin', mixing heroin with cocaine and injecting it into my veins. Cocaine, in those days was highly glamorized in the urban community; it was considered the champaign of drugs. So if you used cocaine you were considered cool or hip! I had just come home from prison, and you would think that I'd learned my lesson from the lifestyle of drug use and crime. However, I knew nothing about the two major components of addiction: progression and tolerance. When I came home from prison, my vocal group, the Silver Stars, got back together. My biological brother joined the group, and we had this Blue Magic and Whispers thing going on, who also had brothers in their acts. We started performing all over the Tri-state area: Newark, New York and Philadelphia. We performed at Carnegie Hall, Chaeta Theatre, RKO proctor and The Garden State Art Center, now the PNC Theatre. The issue was one of the members of the group was the lieutenant of a major drug cartel based out of Newark, NJ and New York, so we had all the drugs we wanted. With the drugs came the women, and with all of this came progression to intravenous drug use, more crime, incarceration and ultimately homelessness.

Progression is best described like this, imagine that you are driving one hundred miles towards the end of a cliff, fifty miles into the drive you stop the car and hang out for a while. Then you get back in the car and travel in the same direction towards the cliff. Progression means that even though I didn't drink or use drugs while I was incarcerated, mentally I hadn't stopped traveling down that road. When I got out and started using again it was as if I never stopped, and more importantly, I was closer to falling off the cliff. Now with progression comes tolerance, which means the more you use the higher your tolerance threshold becomes. One bag was sufficient for euphoria before, now it takes three bags. At first, inhalation is the route, but that's before you learn that intravenous reaches the system quicker. Inhibitions are released and taking risks becomes common place. Now remember earlier I said that addiction is like going through major surgery without anesthesia and being wide awake? I can remember crying and asking Allah, "Why am I going through this?"

The strange thing about heroin or opioid dependence is that it has always been of epidemic proportions in the Black community, but it never got the attention that it's getting today now that predominantly White males are dying from it. It's very strange how racism and affluence are present in every aspect of American society. We must have these discussions if recovery, health and wellness are what we're truly after. There can never be recovery from addiction without a thorough knowledge of self, God and spiritual principles. An even playing field when it comes to therapeutic approaches in treatment is also needed for recovery to be successful. We hear a lot about evidence-based practices and some of those theories and methodologies are useful, but they have to be interpreted and made culturally relevant in order to get to the level of proven practice. The only way to level the playing field in the mental/behavioral health and substance use treatment is that more people in recovery must enter the field and lend their experience to the practice. I believe that this will revolutionize and change the recovery paradigm and produce far greater outcomes. I think that to put treatment into a box and limit its capacity to serve the substance use and mentally ill populous will just continue to exacerbate the problems and continue to waste taxpayer's dollars. Until and unless we allow culturally relative and culturally sensitive practitioners work in a less formalized way, we will continue to Band-Aid the problem and remain in a vicious cycle of failure! We must be open to innovative approaches and discontinue the red lining that is keeping good clinicians out of the field.

Does Behavioral Healthcare really work?

Behavioral Healthcare is a relatively new term that came into being a little over ten years ago. It appears that when the addiction profession merged into the licensing arena with the social workers, etc., the language had to change. Suddenly, it was no longer considered professional to call a heroin addict a junkie or a dope fiend! Ted the wino or drunkard, was referred to as an alcoholic; today he would be referred to as a person with an alcohol use disorder.

So behavioral healthcare is an evolution of the addiction treatment process as I've witnessed over the last thirty plus years, and close to twenty-five years in active addiction. Yep, you guessed it, I started drinking when I was seven or eight years old. Innocently, I was introduced to it by my mother who I love to death. You see, back in those days information wasn't available especially in the Black community. We really had to learn the hard way. One of the biggest jokes I can remember coming up as a child was, "if White people had a cold, Black people had pneumonia." To this day it still appears that the playing field is drastically imbalanced.

So, since the brain is the essence of all behavior, what affects the brain, of course, affects behavior. A brain induced with a psychoactive substance becomes altered and puts the body and the activity of that body into an unhealthy state. This leads to a slow, or sometimes fast, deterioration and destabilization of normal human thinking and functioning. It also leads to jailhouses, institutions or death, spiritually, mentally and physically.

Consequently, behavioral healthcare is mental, physical and spiritual healthcare! What affects one dimension of the human being affects the other. You cannot separate yourself from your mind, body or soul. It is all the same essence. As human beings we are a part of the ecosystem called the universe. The universe as it exists today is made up of nine planets governed by the sun with the assistance of the moon, equaling twelve planets in our solar system. The sun, moon and stars are planets too. Planets are that which are evolved are created from the beginning; whenever that was. When we talk about the twelve steps of recovery that came out of the Oxford Group created by Bill W., and Dr. Bob in the early 1930s, we must understand that regardless to what people feel about Alcoholics and Narcotics Anonymous, the number 12 is very significant. This number I believe, is the reason why what these two gentlemen established out lived them and has transcended space and time and has saved the lives of millions all over the planet. The Twelve Steps and Twelve Traditions. Did you know back in those day alcohol use was a public health crisis and was wreaking havoc on American citizens just as the opioid pandemic is doing today? The government had to step in and prohibit the sale of alcohol. However, a few years later prohibition was repealed, and alcohol became legal and socially acceptable though it continued to wreak havoc on the populous: death by automobile accidents, cirrhosis of the liver, pancreatitis, brain deadness or 'wet brain', high risk sex indulgence, domestic violence, assaults, and reproductive problems.

Did you know that alcohol kills more people annually than all other drugs combined; yet, it is socially acceptable and one of America's richest industries? And it has the most severe withdrawal symptoms. You have to be in a medical facility under 24-hour monitoring by healthcare professionals. Heroin, cocaine and cannabis were my drugs of choice, but alcohol was my drug of dependence, and I thank God for blessing me, after much personal research and development, with the wisdom to know the difference. The best way to explain the difference between drug of choice and drug of dependence is like your choice of a car might be a Mercedes Benz but an Oldsmobile can get you to your destination. I always say, that my best learning was in the streets. We call it Street Corner University! Which brings me back to the number 12.

The root word of university is universe; our universe has 12 planets in it, that we know of right now. We're talking about behavioral healthcare because a healthy mind is a healthy behind as momma use to say! So behavioral health is mental health and mental health starts with the knowledge of self. Now I'm getting ready to go into the spiritual realm of behavioral healthcare, just for a minute, because I know the empirical folks may not like this. These are people who believe everything that happens has to be explained through science and have very little faith in the spiritual and supernatural. However, this is my perspective based on my own personal research and findings in my thirty plus years of practice in the field and twenty plus years of active indulgence and the integration of it all. Check this out! Nine planets, plus the sun, moon and a star (which represents all the stars in the universe, [infinity]), equals 12!

It is recorded that Jesus had twelve disciples. There were twelve tribes of Israel who are said to be God's chosen people, and every clock that we use to tell time has twelve numbers on it! The twelve steps can be broken down into three steps, 1-3, trust in and believe in a power greater than self, let go of E.G.O., (Easing God Out), Step 1, I can't! Step 2, He Can! Step 3, If I Let Him! Steps 4-11 are all about self-analysis which produces self-awareness, becoming rigorously honest, open and willing to change, mending the relationships that you can while establishing new ones. And step 12, helping others, keeping what you have by giving it away, selflessness. Becoming one with the God and humanity.

Once I figured out that the 12 steps in their spiritual significance (God, His chosen people, the disciples) are actually 3 steps, I figured out that the 3 steps refer to the three trimesters it takes to bring a new life in our universe. Nine, in mathematics, represents the number of completion; after the number nine you go to a higher dimension. I'll stop here but what we've discovered is that the 12-step model of recovery is a spiritually and mathematically sound code of conduct that is at the foundation of just about every therapeutic model of thinking and methodology in the field to date.

I think that because of the foundation of the 12-step

program—which is in essence the knowledge of self, God and that which is adverse to good health, natural and sound judgment—I have been empowered to rise up and help myself and countless others to embrace the process of recovery, rehabilitation and resurrection. Yes, behavioral Healthcare works!

The heart of the suggested program of personal recovery is contained in 12 steps describing the experience of the earliest members of the society:

1. We admitted we were powerless over alcohol, that our lives had become unmanageable.

2. Came to believe that a Power greater than ourselves could restore us to sanity.

3. Made a decision to turn our will and our lives over to the care of God as we understood Him.

4. Made a searching and fearless moral inventory of ourselves.

5. Admitted to God, to ourselves and to another human being the exact nature of our wrongs.

6. Were entirely ready to have God remove all these defects of character.

7. Humbly asked Him to remove our shortcomings.

8. Made a list of all persons we had harmed and became willing to make amends to them all.

9. Made direct amends to such people wherever possible, except when to do so would injure them or others.

10. Continued to take personal inventory, and when we were wrong promptly admitted it.

11. Sought through prayer and meditation to improve our conscious contact with God as we understood Him, praying only for knowledge of His will for us and the power to carry that out.

12. Having had a spiritual awakening as the result of these steps, we tried to carry this message to alcoholics and to practice these principles in all our affairs.

The HOW in what makes treatment work is honesty, open-mindedness and willingness to change. This information has opened a God consciousness in me that has given me the power to heal, make the blind see, the deaf hear and the dumb speak, metaphorically speaking. Using myself as the base, I am better able to understand others. I want for them what I want for myself; the inalienable right to the pursuit of happiness, freedom, equity and fairness as a human being regardless to race, class, creed or color.

You will hear me say this time and again throughout this writing, knowledge of self is the basis of everything. It is the foundation upon which any human being can build. If you don't know who you are, your origin in the world, your history and your heredity, then you're like a ship on high seas without a destination, without a guide and no rudder. You will be taken by the winds of time to wherever, whenever. I'm suggesting that once a person has a thorough knowledge and understanding of themselves, their history and heredity, they can get to the exact nature of whatever is ailing them and heal. This resolve is not as simple as it sounds, because it requires fearlessness, daring to be different and firm resolve. It took over thirty years to get to this plane of understanding, actually forty years, as I told you I went through hell with eyes wide open and only the scientists understand what I'm saying here.

The difference between Use, Abuse and Dependence

The disease of substance use disorder is a chronic illness much like sugar diabetes. Everybody who eats a lot of sugar, starches and fatty foods doesn't become diabetic, nor does everybody who drinks alcohol and/or uses psychoactive substances, pain medication or other drugs develop dependency, addiction or substance use disorder. If you review the Jellinek Curve chart that I introduced in this book you will see the progressive nature of addiction from use to abuse to dependence. When a person reaches the dependency stage of substance use disorder his/her life becomes totally unmanageable and out of control. Rational thinking and sound judgement become impaired and erratic, and high-risk behavior becomes the norm. Employment, relationships and socialization become critically disrupted. The pressures of life seem to become more and more unbearable leading to self-harm and/or harm to someone else.

There are stages of evolution in addiction, and this evolution is inclusive of genetic, hereditary, environmental and many other factors that must be taken into consideration when we talk about use, abuse and dependence. The point is that each stage builds on the next, and the ultimate end is the same so why chance it? I started out a social drinker, smoker and user. I went from use to abuse rapidly and dependence just as quick; in fact, I may have skipped use and abuse and went straight to dependence. For some of us, because of an element known as predisposition, go straight to dependence. Predisposition means that the possibility and probability of addiction is extremely high because of genetic factors such as a parent or grandparent who may have a chemical dependency problem. A person can also be predisposed to an environment i.e., a high crime, poor socioeconomic neighborhood where psychoactive drug sales is almost commonplace and glamorized. It can also be an economically rich environment where cocktails, wine and prescription medication can lead to chemical dependency. The bottom line is that addiction untreated has only three outcomes, institutions, jailhouses and death. There are two main elements in the disease of addiction whether a person is rich or poor or in between, Black, White, male or female, Christian, Muslim or Jew, no matter what culture, these two elements are progression and tolerance. And the GAS that fuels the disease of addiction is Guilt, Anger and Shame! When I learned to understand, study and master these concepts or elements of the illness, recovery became more and more ubiquitous.

Are people who become dependent on drugs or alcohol weak or evil people?

Alcoholism and drug addiction are chronic diseases just like cancer, sugar diabetes and cirrhosis of the liver. These are all chronic illnesses and must be treated with proper medicinal protocols, nutrition, cognitive reframing, behavioral and environmental modification.

Sickness is not a moral deformity or spiritual weakness; however, morality and spirituality are extremely important aspects of health, wellness and the recovery process. I read in a book entitled *How To Eat To Live* by Mr. Elijah Muhammad that most sickness comes from what we eat and drink. He said that this means what we eat mentally and physically. And this is true, because we cannot ignore the cognitive impairment associated with the disease of addiction and alcoholism. By this I mean that the normal functioning of the brain and mind becomes impaired and imbalanced so much so that wrong becomes right and the propensity to take chances and do that which you may not do under normal circumstances becomes easy. The lifestyle, the culture, the language, the imagery, environment; every aspect of active addiction must be abated or decreased over time for full sustain remission to happen. Similarly, to keep one's sugar levels under control there are certain foods that must be avoided at all costs, and an entirely new attitude must be adopted and maintained for sustained health and wellness. Constant monitoring must take place to prevent relapse.

This concept was revealed to me in the detoxification phase of my recovery. This happened for me at Elizabeth General Hospital. The program was called The Seton Center. I later learned that this was the hospital where my eldest sibling and only sister, was born. My sister was the woman of both my social and spiritual birth (I'll have to explain this at another time, probably my next book). But it was at this phase of my recovery (detox) that I heard and embraced the concept of the disease of addiction and alcoholism; that was thirty-three years ago, and I have not looked back since. There's been some bumps in the road, rough times and setbacks. But I also learned in recovery that a setback is nothing but a set-up for a comeback, and in most cases, your comeback is even stronger.

Unless one can admit that there is a problem, there can be no healing. Usually the addict is the last to realize that he/she is sick because he/she doesn't see it. I refer to this as the 'blind state'. In clinical terminology it is referred to as denial. This is the state when everyone in the addict's life can see that something is wrong because of his/her indulgence in substance use and/or drinking but the addict him/herself. Because substance use decreases inhibitions and tends to lead to an alter ego state lending to extremely high-risk behaviors, poor judgment and negative associations. Consequently, relationships become estranged, employment affected, and human dysfunction becomes commonplace.

None of the above can be categorized as weakness and or evil; it is the nature of the individual who suffers from the disease of addiction. You will come across, in this writing, the phrase, Dr. Jekyll and Mr. Hyde. Two extraordinary parts of the same human being. In other words, a person under the influence of alcohol and/or substance use enters an altered state. The brain's chemistry is changed to the point that thoughts and behaviors become completely opposite of those of the same individual in a sober state. The shy person becomes bold and bodacious, the fearful and timid person becomes brave, the person who is normally moral and upright, becomes conniving and mischievous; hence the phrase, Dr. Jekyll and Mr. Hyde.

So, the alcohol and substance use disorders are recognized as chronic brain diseases with certain pathology like any other chronic illness. Some of its symptoms are: dishonesty, distrust, disruptive, distractive, discombobulated, distasteful and disabled. We can go on and on with the list, but I think you get the point here. Excessive alcohol and/or substance use can destroy your life. But the disorder does not in and of itself constitute that the person suffering is a weak person trying to be good, or an evil person trying to become righteous. Instead they're a sick person trying to get well. Chronic means that the disease cannot be cured but can be effectively treated, managed and persons can enter into full sustained remission.

Is substance use and mental illness hereditary?

According to most research that's out there the answer is 50/50! Much of what we learn and do is an equal amount of hereditary and environmental. The problem with heredity, as it relates to substance use and mental disorder specifically amongst Blacks and people of color, is that their genetic structure has been severely altered from the experience of slavery in America. The brutal process of breeding, breaking and detaching a people from their origin in the world and stripping them of the knowledge of self: their names, God, religion, the norms and mores of their ancestors, has serious implications on the molecular level. Then you force on them foreign culture: norms, mores, names, God and religion, and label them Negroes, which means something dead or lifeless. They are told that they are three fifths of a human being and you have them refer to you as Master! They are given a White Jesus Christ, White Mother Mary, White Angels and White Disciples at the last supper. You indoctrinate them to believe that any and everything Black is bad, no good or ugly; black cat equals bad luck; blackmail is synonymous to corruption or bribery; blackball is to ban or debar. We were made to work for free for three hundred plus years, and then emancipated without being given any resources to stay free! Plus, there was no therapy, no mental debriefing or cognitive reframing and no plan for us to ever recover.

Adversely to do something like this to a whole nation of people could be hereditary mental illness too. To think that you're better, smarter, superior to another because of the whiteness of your skin is a disease as well. So, there is an inherent or hereditary aspect of mental illness and substance use disorder far beyond the inducement of psychoactive substances. Do you know that at some point in time in the *Diagnostical Statistical Manual* there was a diagnosis for a slave who wanted to be free and constantly ran away from the plantation?

There is much to be considered when we talk about substance use disorder and mental illness in this country. The treatment paradigm must be culturally sensitive and that's the importance of writing this chapter. If you haven't walked in my footsteps, then you don't have a clue about how I feel. It boggles my mind that White professionals seem to feel that they have the solution to Black people's problems; and I would suggest that Black people feel that they have the solution to White people's problems, but neither of them seems to be willing to have this type of discussion. It has been my experience that most professionals want to skip over the slave, slave master scenario as if it never happened. Whites don't want to talk about it, though they benefit from it, and Blacks don't want to talk about it because they're hoping that someday things will change, and we'll all live together happily ever after. And those of us asking for healthy, honest discussion and reflection are considered rocking the boat and/or opening old wounds. Historically in this country and beyond Black people have proven their ability to nurse, nourish, educate, counsel and heal people of all nations and cultures.

So, when we look at heredity as it relates to mental health and substance use disorder, I think of the term cognitive dissonance. This is a psychosis that refers to a situation involving conflicting attitudes, beliefs or behaviors. This produces a feeling of discomfort leading to an alteration in one of the attitudes, beliefs or behaviors to reduce the discomfort and restore balance. One of the chief elements in the disease of addiction is the desire to reduce discomfort. The societal discomfort of classism, racism and materialism wherein there are two Americas, rich and poor, Black and White, Separate and Unequal. Until justice reigns supreme there will never be any true peace, true recovery or true health and wellness for all.

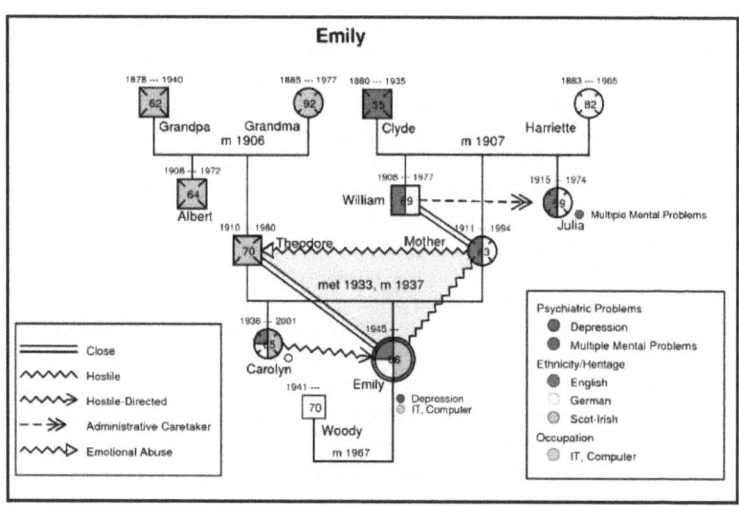

Does the government have something to do

with the problem of substance use disorder?

The brightest lights in the urban community at night are the neon lights on the liquor stores. Alcohol use disorder causes more sickness, public safety concerns and deaths than all the other psychoactive substances combined. It also has the most chronic withdrawal. The glamorization of alcohol use and psychoactive substance use, specifically heroin, cocaine and cannabis on billboards, television ads and movies is wreaking havoc in our communities.

In 1989, Oliver North, a national security aide in the Reagan-Bush administration, was convicted on three felony counts connected to the Iran-Contra controversy. This involved the United States government secretly selling arms to Iran, in breach of an embargo at the time. The dual purpose was to coax the Iranian regime to free US hostages while using the proceeds to skirt a ban and fund Contra guerrillas who were fighting the leftwing government in Nicaragua. North's convictions were later overturned on a technicality.

Ronald Reagan had been cleared by a congressional commission of orchestrating a cover-up in what also came to be called Irangate in 1987. Several top government officials were convicted, including the national security advisers, John Poindexter and Robert MacFarlane, as well as the assistant secretary of state, Elliot Abrams. Poindexter's conviction was overturned on similar grounds to North's, while MacFarlane and Abrams received pardons from President George H. W. Bush.

The above is just the tip of the iceberg when it comes to the government's involvement in substance use disorder. Some of my Black consumers have commented that if psychoactive drugs and alcohol were good for them, they'd have to march on Washington, DC with picket signs to access them. The disproportionality of substance use disorder and substance use related incarceration as it pertains to Black and White people in this country is well documented. 75% of the prison population has a substance use and/or mental health disorder, and 65% of the total prison population in America are Black and Brown people. However, I have noticed that there is a commonality when it comes to the principles of treatment as long as it is culturally sensitive.

In talking about diseases as riveting and extreme as substance use disorder and mental illness the solutions must be equally as extreme and cover many cultural and socio-economic standards. Governmental and political factors must be included in the regimen for sustained health and wellness which is the goal of treatment, in other words government must take responsibility in assisting in the treatment process on all level, legislation, funding, etc. When the governance of a people turns its back on the needs, concerns, health and welfare of its citizenry, it's just a matter of time before it crumbles and falls. History best rewards our research and as Uncle Yah Yah says, one example is better than thousands of books of illustrations.

Just a few centuries ago it was boasted that the sun would never set on the British Empire and it fell. It fell because of its great neglect of the needs and aspirations of its poor and depraved citizenry. When ancient Rome fell from grace it was due to its unwillingness to provide for its sick and disenfranchised citizens. The solution to social ills, sicknesses and diseases throughout the annals of history always seems to come from the people or person least likely to have it. He never comes from the dominant class of his contemporaries, the rich, the educated, the politicians or journalists. Nope! Usually he comes from the unwanted, rejected and despised. His ability to analyze and sift through what hasn't worked for the populous and to bring to surface that which does is an inner spirit endowed upon him by the creator. To integrate the spiritual, mental, physical, positive and negative he produces a serum, formula or model that works.

The 1980s was a very interesting decade in America; there were so many interesting things that happened during this period. Terry Gorski is a scientist and scholar in the field of behavioral healthcare. His main focus is on relapse prevention and he introduced a model of treatment to address the psychological and addiction needs of incarcerated persons returning to the community that actually works! It is reported that he spoke to legislatures, lobbyists, and other treatment providers in Washington, DC and was rejected and indiscriminately run out of town. It is further reported that these leaders were an integral part of the beginning of the Prison Industrial Complex and were not interested in a treatment paradigm that could interfere with their plans. The treatment modality Mr. Gorski introduced is known as 'PICS', Post/Pre-Incarceration Syndrome. I use it in my clinical practice, and it works with some of the most so-called, incorrigible felons! PICS for a person returning home from prison is comparable to Post Traumatic Stress Disorder (PTSD) in a person returning home from the military who has been in a war zone or in combat. The two have very similar pathologies. As such the need for support and treatment for social readjustment back into "normal society" is necessary.

I'm not necessarily a conspiracy theorist, but I do believe that the government can do more in the way of prevention and treatment of addiction and mental illness. In fact, I think it should be a priority since it affects countless numbers of persons and their families. Addiction chronically impacts the economy in lost wages, employee productivity, accidents, medical costs and crime.

What are the signs and symptoms of substance and/or alcohol use disorder?

Here we want to talk about prevention/intervention. As they say, an ounce of prevention is better than a pound of cure. For the most part the Jellinek Curve gives you signs and symptoms of the disease of addiction, and it breaks it down into three phases: early onset, crucial and chronic. Intervention, treatment and recovery can happen at any phase in this cycle and can only be successfully administered by a clinician who knows and understands what phase the consumer is in.

The clinician must utilize effective interventions and strategies to move the consumer into the phases of remission which has three to four stages: early partial remission, early remission, full partial remission, and full sustained remission. Each stage builds on the next much like active addiction. Rarely does a person enter right into the chronic phase of the illness, though it is possible. I've heard many of the consumers we treat say that for them it was love at first drink or use. This means that from their first psychoactive indulgence they were off to the races. Like a Porsche automobile, from 0 to 100 in seconds.

I will from time to time continue to talk about

tolerance and progression. Because often, persons who become dependent start off innocently. Substance use disorder is subtle, insidious, cunning and baffling. Things to watch for are unattended resentment, guilt and shame.

People deal with resentment in three ways: aggressively, assertively or passive aggressively. If this mindset is not addressed therapeutically, resentment turns into anger and becomes volatile. At that point something must be done to relieve the pressure. Guilt and shame have the same psychological effects, and the heightened emotional sensitivity must also be relieved.

So, research teaches that what we don't talk about and attempt to ignore becomes repressed material. And the more we repress or deny, the further detached we become from what is real and/or normal and who we really are. We become emotionally constipated, our psychological growth is stunted and we become stuck. Then comes external stimuli.

My father used to say to me, "Boy, it's not the things that you do, it's the company you keep!" I hate to say it, but he was right. As human beings there is a natural yearning for human interaction called relationships; and again, another cliché is, birds of a feather, flock together. Therefore, another warning sign of substance use disorder is peer relationships, friends, lovers, associates and family members.

You may think that to be an alcoholic one would have to be hanging around a fire lit garbage can in the cold, drinking wine all day and night. But that isn't so; we're on court benches, riding in police patrol cars, college students, morticians, doctors, nurses; people from all walks of life suffer from alcohol abuse. But they keep company with like-minded people and ultimately, they began to isolate. There are many more subtle signs of alcohol and psychoactive substance dependence, and they are as varied as the people who have them. Bottom line is that the disease is chronic and must be treated that way.

How can substance use disorder be prevented?

Imagine being a Black child growing up in a family of total chaos and dysfunction. Your father, the sole breadwinner, thinks that he's drinking socially because he works during the week. He goes out on weekends and spends his money on gambling, women and getting drunk. He feels that he's earned the right to do so because his boss had him working on the job like a slave with little pay and no benefits. Now he comes home broke, and Mom has been struggling all week to feed her six or seven children that he helped to produce. Maybe not all of them, because while Dad was so busy sowing his royal oats someone else could have caught mother depressed, feeling rejected and neglected and felt that he was doing everybody a favor by slipping in. If even on one occasion the child witnesses this, and the mother thinks the child is too young to know what's going on, it creates an atmosphere of distrust and delusion.

Added to this, the father and mother (husband and wife, 'til death do they part) are fighting and the child, a toddler, is witnessing this too. What happens to the psyche? The self-esteem? Added to this, the child is constantly being physically punished by the mother, bordering on child abuse, because he reminds her of the father either in character, appearance or behaviors. Now the child could be acting out because of what he's being exposed to. The confusion, the chaos, and the violence. Fear, shame and even guilt sets in. The child begins to think, am I causing this? He feels victimized, oppressed, and wants to escape!

The families he's watching on television are all White: *Leave it to Beaver*, *The Brady Bunch*, *Bonanza* and they seem to be fine, no problems there, except with *Bonanza*, a single White male is raising three sons in the wild west. But even that is just an interesting family dynamic. Then I guess somebody came up with the bright idea that we needed to add some color to the family TV profile, and they came out with shows like *Good Times*, *Sanford and Son*, and they even went as far as to add interracial relationships to the fray with *The Jeffersons*, and then came *The Bill Cosby Show*! Now todays family's media profile has an entirely different, and in many ways more dysfunctional dynamic, and the producers are trying to make this dysfunction more acceptable.

The point of this in preventing substance use disorder is that prevention starts at home, with the family, and deeper than that, with every individual in a family, community, neighborhood, society, government, and nation. Everyone must play a part. The disease of substance use disorder does not matter if you're Black or White, rich or poor, married or single. It is an equal opportunity destroyer like any other viruses looking for a host to get in and break down the immune system. And because of the universality of its causative factors, prevention must be equally aggressive and comprise a multidisciplinary approach.

We have a broken healthcare system wherein the so-called health providers act like gang bangers jockeying for turf! Social workers are poised as superior to professional counselors, and addiction counselors are the lowest on the totem pole. Psychologists, psychiatrists and physicians all have their specialties; one thinking they are more significant than the other. Yet they are all seeing the same consumers. They are so focused on promoting their discipline while the consumer base continues to increase and die simultaneously, because it seems to be about how much money can be made rather than how many lives can be saved.

The healthcare industry, for the most part, is driven by insurance companies and as a result we have a sick nation. According to Wikipedia, health care in the United States is provided by many distinct organizations. Healthcare facilities are largely owned and operated by private sector businesses. 58% of US community hospitals are non-profit, 21% are government owned, and 21% are for-profit. According to the World Health Organization (WHO), the United States spent more on healthcare per capita ($9,403), and more on healthcare as a percentage of its GDP (17.1%), than any other nation in 2014.

Despite being among the top world economic powers, the US remains the sole industrialized nation in the world without universal healthcare coverage.

In 2013, 64% of health spending was paid for by the government, and funded via programs such as Medicare, Medicaid, the Children's Health Insurance Program, and the Veterans Health Administration. People aged under 67 acquire insurance via their or a family member's employer, by purchasing health insurance on their own, or are uninsured. Health insurance for public sector employees is primarily provided by the government in its role as employer.

The United States life expectancy is 78.6 years at birth, up from 75.2 years in 1990; this ranks 42nd among 224 nations, and 22nd out of the 35 industrialized OECD countries, down from 20th in 1990. In 2016 and 2017 life expectancy in the U.S. dropped for the first time since 1993. Of 17 high-income countries studied by the National Institutes of Health, the United States in 2013 had the highest or near-highest prevalence of obesity, car accidents, infant mortality, heart and lung disease, sexually transmitted infections, adolescent pregnancies, injuries, and homicides. A 2014 survey of the healthcare systems of 11 developed countries found the US healthcare system to be the most expensive and worst-performing in terms of health access, efficiency, and equity.

My approach for decades has been to bring families, friends and all professional entities together in promoting the health and welfare of the consumer. However, it has not been easy getting the cooperation necessary, so innovation, creativity, eclecticism and a do-for-self mindset has been my practice and curriculum, and it works. Preventive healthcare must be all-inclusive. It will take the cooperation of families and all government entities, politics, academicians, religion and media. Without this all-inclusive approach, divisiveness among disciplines will continue to worsen the problem. Again, an ounce of prevention is better than a pound of cure. More on this will be discussed later as it relates to food and drinks.

Is there such a thing as social substance use?

In my professional opinion, social substance use is like being half pregnant. The fact is that either you're pregnant or you're not! Substance use is a part of substance use disorder like A, B and C are a part of the alphabet. It amazes me how alcohol use has become a part of America's cultural norm. That which was once considered the scourge of society causing legislation to be implemented to stop the sale of it has now become glamorized and is considered the hallmark of socialization and sophistication.

I remember as a teenager walking down the street in Newark, NJ, the town of my birth. I grew up in the projects with four brothers and a sister. My father was a blue-collar worker and fisherman; the sole provider of the family. Moms was a home maker/housewife and believe you me, she was a heck of a disciplinarian. So, I'm walking down the street and I see this billboard of a well-groomed, sophisticated looking Black couple; the brother has on a tuxedo, the sister has on a beautiful white gown, and they're both smiling with pearly white teeth. It looks as if they're dancing, swaying to a real serious groove. They appear to be extremely happy and having a wonderful time. Next to them on a table is a bottle of Jack Daniels liquor and two glasses with ice in them; and the ice is sparkling. The caption on the billboard reads, 'Taste the Pleasure!' There's a term in psychology known as subliminal seduction, which means to subtly suggest something to someone that ultimately becomes a part of the persons psyche, character and persona. This is done without the person ever realizing that they've been seduced. So, whenever I felt sad, unhappy or depressed, I'd think about the billboard and even though I couldn't afford Jack Daniels, Boone's Farm Apple Wine, Thunderbird or Colt 45 were sufficient. Then I'd look for some female to complete the image. Now of course, back then I didn't know this but as they say, hindsight is 20/20.

Now here's the opposite extreme, I had a consumer I was counseling, and he said, "Dr., you don't understand what it's like to be a young adult walking down the streets looking at a billboard and not being able to understand what it's saying because you can't read!" By opposite I mean here's and individual who can't read at all, yet he still suffered from the disease of addition. The young man had to be in his mid to late 20s! Today that young man is a successful businessman and contributes a major portion of his salary to youth initiatives and teenage literacy.

Uncle Yah Yah says that universal travel is 360 degrees and that all things travel in their opposites. So, you can't know what's right until you know what's wrong; you can't get up, if you've never been down, and you can't know what a smooth road is like unless you have a bumpy one to compare it with. Therefore, the first step in recovery is admittance and acceptance. Once the issue has been identified, it is no longer a mystery. The key is to meet the person wherever they are on the continuum of care.

Does substance use affect your creativity and ability to master certain skills?

Because most psychoactive substances effect the brain in such a way that most inhibitions are released, it is misinterpreted by persons who use these substances as the ultimate source of creativity and skill mastery. I can remember thinking that I couldn't function and/or deal with life without the use of some drug or drink. Family dysfunction, poverty, poor housing, poor education, political/judicial/religious corruption, pimping social programs, no jobs and easy access to psychoactive substances, guns, criminality and sex have produced generations of broken families. Broken families include single parent households (predominantly women), substance use disorders, sexually transmitted diseases, and other co-morbid illnesses, illiteracy, unemployability, hopelessness, helplessness and homelessness.

Then you have the other side of the spectra: affluenza, privilege, easy access to wealth, healthcare, success, egotism, sexism, racism also leads to substance use disorder due to the desire to escape. In this case the pressures to maintain a certain level of status and privilege can become overwhelming and easy access to psychoactive or even prescription medication can lead to substance use disorder. The point is, no matter what side of the spectrum you come from true creativity comes from within and it cannot be made up of matter that already exists. To create means to bring something into existence that did not exist. It's a natural phenomenon that requires no external influences.

I have treated many consumers who have informed me of research they have done to produce the chemical composition needed to bring about the euphoria they wanted. It is the euphoria that persons with substance use disorder believe to be the impetus for their creativity and ability to cope. The problem is, there is no sustainability in this lifestyle. The lifestyle of substance use disorder is so delusional, stressful and pretentious that once you cross the threshold into dependence the cycle is stupendous.

Several of our most popular entertainers are affected by substance use disorder on various levels. The first that comes to mind describes her performance on stage as her alter ego! Could her creativity be driven by psychoactive substance or alcohol? Another famous entertainer, possibly intoxicated from fame, altered his appearance to the point that he became all but unrecognizable by family, friends and fans. It appears that substance use, though he was rich and famous, caused us to suffer his loss. We suffered the loss of another one of our shining stars, who was considered one of the most golden voices of the 80s, 90s and into the 21st century. And the list goes on and on and on. The stresses of not understanding the high lifestyle of substance use disorder has caused us much grief.

When I think about creativity and mastery, I think of the Creator and His creation. It seems to me that for Him to create the universe, He had to be 100% in accord with His own nature and the nature of everything around Him. The Bible says, in the beginning there was total darkness and out of that darkness, He brought forth light. This means He had to master the darkness first. To master means to have great skill or proficiency. This requires knowledge and the ability to apply knowledge, which is called wisdom, and out of wisdom comes understanding. So, knowledge is power, and it gives its inherent that ability to create, recreate and master his/her destiny. However, some of us are unwilling to search out and apply the necessary knowledge that will enable us to recreate and recover. Once we become willing to accept requisite knowledge for our own situation and circumstance, and only then, can we attain the power necessary to free ourselves of the things that hold us hostage. As the scripture says, the Truth shall set you free! We have already said, recovery requires rigorous honesty, you can't get any truer than that

What is it like to perform before thousands of people sober?

It is true that psychoactive substances including and, in many cases, exclusively alcohol, affects the brain functioning in such a way that it alters consciousness, releases inhibitions, reduces shyness, and enables behavior that would not have ordinarily been exhibited under normal circumstances. Many dancers, singers, musicians, writers, producers, publishers and managers use drugs and alcohol to do what they do. For the most part it is considered the norm in the music industry; to not indulge can cause ostracism and exclusion.

When I was around 11 or 12 years old, I was in a singing group called the Del Quapries and we were performing with a band (the Soul Knights) in a talent contest at the Carnegie Hall Theatre in New York City! Man, being a young poverty-stricken Black male from Newark, that was big time for me. We were smoking weed, poppin' pills, and drinking cough syrup; we thought we were having a good ol' time! We won the contest which meant the opportunity to perform at the Garden State Art Center now known as the PNC, Performing Arts Center, in Holmdel, NJ. We performed before thousands but because of substance use the group's business was mismanaged. Our manager had an alcohol use problem also. So, after about five years of performing the chitterling circuit, with all the money we earned going to management for expenses, uniforms, equipment, and house furniture the group began to break up. Our parents would constantly question us about the money, before the break-up but we were having such a great time! To us, at that time, wine, drugs, women and songs were everything; the lot of the prodigal son! Little did I know, I was destined to become a feeder of swine and husker of corn and chemically dependent, but I did. We continued the vocal portion of the group but before my 16th birthday, I was on my way to prison for a conspiracy to commit murder charge.

I was a popular prep school student, potentially an all-city athlete, and professional entertainer but in less than five years I was in jail. What was at the root of it all? Substance use disorder and mental illness. Throughout my childhood I had symptoms of depression and anxiety that went undiagnosed until I went to treatment at the age of 29. The stigma of mental illness, being called crazy, taken advantage of and being looked down on as weak, was much more severe in those days and treatment protocols weren't as varied. I masked it, and because of this, recovery came the hard way. I only focused on the psychoactive substance use disorder and its pathology. Subsequently, I learned that unconsciously I'd determined that self-medicating was the best way of dealing with my mental illness. Once I realized this and decided to stop, I would not need medication anymore. It wasn't easy, and more importantly, it did not come without internal and external support. I had to make myself understand that relapse and recovery co-exist, and because the disease is chronic, recovery is 24/7 365.

I came to realize that since addiction and mental illness was most pronounced in the physiological its essence had to exist in the metaphysical and/or spiritual realm. I really began to examine the 12 Steps of Alcoholics Anonymous, and I began to incorporate them into my life. I studied and memorized each step. I worked them with a sponsor that I still have to this day. Funny story, and I always joke about this. When I came out of rehab (twenty-one days of inpatient rehabilitation program) and was told that I should get a sponsor, I chose four; one for each side of me: right, left, front and back. I was serious about not going back. Which recalls the story of Prophet Lot in the Bible, when he told his family and followers, "Don't turn back!" This history also gives insight into the possibility of losing your own family to this disease. There's nothing you can do if they refuse the help. Lot's wife turned back! Did you know that some researchers say, that alcoholism started with Prophet Noah!

Today I am an independent, classic soul artist performing with a vocal group (quartet) known as the Silver Stars and we have performed all over the country and we've even performed in Africa, sober. We're still together, recording and growing that business. The act has been together for forty years now; the first eight years were traumatic to say the least (that's another book) but suffice it to say we survived. Two of the original members of the group passed away and for a while we travelled and performed as a trio; last year we added a new member. So, yeah there is life after addiction and mental illness. We do recover.

Do artists need drugs and/or alcohol to perform or create material?

I can remember in early recovery when I could not conceive living life without the use of some type of stimulant or depressant. I thought to myself, *well it's okay if I just smoke weed, you see, because it's that heroin and cocaine that really gets me into trouble. I could probably even drink a little wine every now and then too.* They call this stinkin' thinkin'! At that time, I knew nothing about substitutions or the difference between substance of preference and substance of dependence. When I learned this, it changed my perspective and deepened my new-found quest for knowledge (recovery).

The glamorization of substance and alcohol use in the entertainment industry is overwhelming. It's as much a part of the culture as apple pie is to American! Party, party, party, Academy Awards, Grammy Awards, Golden Globe Awards, BET & MTV Awards, any excuse to party and drink and use drugs. To be creative means relating to or involving the imagination or original ideas, especially in the production of an artistic work. This is something that every human being is born with, but it has been standardized and framed in such a way that most artists have been marginalized. Industry moguls force them to create a social construct that is destabilizing to certain populous in American society. In other words, for the most part, todays artists and their artistic talents are being used to dumb down the public.

The American entertainment industry is being used to create a fictitious image that everything is okay in a time of peril. They make alcohol and drug use easily accessible and socially acceptable. The beat of the music and the lyrics have a debilitating affect, and therefore creativity must fit into a certain mode to be promoted and distributed by the major record companies, publishers and agents. Therefore, true originality and creativity is discouraged along with the natural and wholesome lifestyle that engenders true creativity. Artists are made to compromise core principles and values in order to become successful. As a result, they suffer cognitive dissonance, meaning they are made to mentally justify their errant behavior by putting the blame on the person ill affected by their conduct, which is a major contributor to substance use disorder and/or mental illness.

Imagine growing up in the projects, poor and destitute barely surviving, and all you see on television is basketball, football and baseball players earning multimillion-dollar contracts. Boxers, entertainers, rappers and movie stars are earning the same. They are living lavishly and wearing all the latest styles. Now here you are trying to fit into a social construct that has been socially and psychologically engineered to be the be all and end all of modernity. If you're not with it you're ostracized, considered an outcast, misfit or, as they said in the ol days, a corn ball! So, since you can't keep up with the Joneses, what do you do? Cognitive dissonance, you drink, drug and you create your own reality. Very few people know how to use despair to give expression to hope and ultimate prosperity. It has been said that some of the most profound, creative and prolific ideas, have been born out of the darkest, dullest, gloomiest situations and circumstances. I mentioned earlier that I was taught by my mentor and spirit guide that the universal travel of thought is 360 degrees, and as such you cannot know what's right if you don't know what's wrong. You can't know what's up if you've never been down, and you can't know what a smooth road is without a bumpy one to compare it to.

My spirit guide has taught me that knowledge is a free man, not bound by any institution of learning. Not Harvard, Oxford or Yale! Knowledge permits its bearer to expand boundaries, overcome barriers and reach unlimited heights. To me, this is true creativity. As a clinician and entertainer, I find myself integrating these fields into my practice, and the results have been phenomenal. I think that creativity must come from a natural source to be genuine. So, it stands to reason that from the Creator comes creativity. Not from drugs, alcohol or some other external stimuli.

What is an example of being a functioning drug addict?

I was working in a laboratory as a technician. I was talking to one of the chemists who'd noticed a black scar on my arm that looked like the type of track that an intravenous drug user would have on his or her arm. This was one of the best paying jobs that I'd had in those days. We were testing food for salmonella and E-coli bacteria. We were also testing pool water and sludge. On the other side I was selling weed and pills; the strange thing is, though I made money, I eventually became my best customer.

Anyway, the chemist and I started hangin' out and he introduced me to mainlining, shooting up, and intravenous drug use. Before long, I was strung out and heroin use dependent. I overdosed twice; the second time I did it, as I was losing consciousness, I could hear the chemist, saying, "I'll never bring that m*#ther F*#ker with me again!"

In those days if a person overdosed or died the people with him/her would not call 911 or wait around because they feared being arrested. I can remember seeing a dead body taken out of a shooting gallery and dumped in an alley way. Anyway, when they brought me back around and into full consciousness, I can remember saying to myself, *that was the best high I ever had!* That's the insanity of substance use disorder. I believe at that point, I was at the apex of my illness. Shortly thereafter, I was kicked out of my parents' house and I became homeless. Which I believe in hindsight is the best thing that could've ever happened. Don't get me wrong, I had the best parents a Black male child could have growing up in urban America in the 50s, 60s and 70s. My father was the son of a slave and had served in the military. He was born in Alabama, and after the military he worked and moved his mother, daughter, brother and sister to New Jersey. Shortly thereafter, his sister was murdered by a jealous boyfriend who also killed himself in my grandmother's home.

My father's father was killed, while on the job, prior to my father going to the military. A White crane operator dropped a heavy object on his head. I can't remember the details, but I can recall feeling very bitter when my father was telling me the story. My father was the nicest guy in the world until he became intoxicated; when that happened, the house went into turmoil. As such, I was exposed to domestic violence as a child and therefore developed a very fragile, fearful and shame-based character.

My mother is a very beautiful woman from South Carolina, and one of the sweetest people you'd ever want to meet. She came from a very large family of singers. I mean my mother's family could *sing*; all her brothers and sisters had beautiful voices. They produced children who are singers and have had some very lucrative and successful careers such as the great gospel performer and artist John P. Kee, Leon Nelson who performed with the Drifters, Moe Kee who performs with Blue Magic, my brother Alkhalique (Keith Kee Hamilton) and myself. Mom was an entertainer; she performed with the likes of Sarah Vaughn and Cissy Houston (Whitney Houston's mother) before she married, became pregnant and a homemaker for my father. I guess she was happy in the beginning, and more importantly, she stayed true to her vows; she stayed with my father until he passed away and never remarried. At 87 years old, she is managing Alzheimer's disorder, and she's still as beautiful as ever. My S-hero!

I can remember feeling very insecure about my ethnicity and my complexion as a young boy; from about six or seven years old and into my teens. It was a time of great racial strife and social change. I was eleven years old at the time of the Newark rebellion, and there were riots taking place all over the country. Black people were sick and tired of third-class citizenship and were beginning to lash out! I'm looking at this through clear lenses today, because at that time I was so intoxicated by some substance; I don't know how I survived. All I know is that I was trying to escape from violence, resentment, shame, poverty and an environment that was diametrically opposed to my very existence.

Dr. Joy Degruy, who is an internationally renowned researcher, educator, author and lecturer, talks about Post Traumatic Slave Syndrome and how the vestiges of slavery impact our lives and experiences to this day. She compared Post Traumatic Slave Syndrome to Post Traumatic Stress Disorder, and she asked the question why didn't Black people ever receive clinical intervention or therapy? As I reviewed some of her work, I couldn't help but to agree that past trauma, depending on its severity, must be addressed in therapy. If not, it can and will lead to long term emotional and mental disability and substance use disorder. It's hard trying to survive when you don't know yourself or your origin in the world. Without such knowledge you have no starting point or foundation to build upon. I presented an illustration of a genogram in this book, and I will go into more detail of the genogram in future writings. As a Black male professional in long term recovery, I can't tell you how important knowing who you are is in the therapeutic process of health and wellness. And the sad thing is that most Blacks in America have been made to frown on treatment, therapy and/or counseling. Treatment has been stigmatized and made unattractive while substance use has been glamorized and made very attractive. In order to change this, we have to re-educate, motivate and rehabilitate.

What approach do you take when dealing with mental disorder or substance use dependence?

There are many schools of thought as it relates to recovery, remission, health and wellness. It reminds me of what my spirit guide says in *Uncle Yah Yah 21st Century Man of Wisdom*, "There are as many ways to see a thing as there are people who see it!" My approach to therapy is eclectic and that is what makes me so effective. I meet the client where they're at and I let them drive the process. I use whatever interventions that are most effective for that individual; it may be cognitive behavioral therapy, behavior modification, rational emotive therapy, gestalt therapy, brief therapy, didactic, motivational enhancement therapy, grief and trauma therapy, dialectic therapy, anger management, and the list goes on and on. Most of the time it's just reflective listening and summarization. Helping the consumers defragment and put his/her thoughts into perspective.

I also promote healthy diet and exercise in my practice. You are what you eat; therefore, if one is ever going to get to the point of self-actualization proper nutrition is of the utmost importance. Physical fitness goes hand in hand with proper nutrition; you cannot be physically fit with a poor diet. It's like being in the middle of the ocean with a weight around your neck; it won't work.

As three-dimensional creatures, the human being is mind, body and spirit, and each aspect is affected by substance use, neurological deficiency and/or mental illness. Therefore, treatment must focus on all three planes of existence; otherwise, you can't have a balance. A multidisciplinary approach is the most effective; its synonymous with the concept, "it takes a village to raise a child!" Every discipline in the health care industry must be involved. If the person has legal issues, the judiciary needs to be involved; if it's homelessness, hunger and/or finance, the office of social services and welfare must be involved. If the person is unemployed, vocational rehab and employment needs to be involved. The clinician must be skilled in accessing these resources, linking the consumer to these resources and following up to maintain the continuity of care.

The consumer also needs to develop, establish and maintain a positive social support system to sustain ongoing recovery and to prevent relapse. Full sustained remission for substance use disorder is usually determined in twelve months, when there are no signs of symptoms of the illness. However, there are other schools of thought that propose that recovery is a lifelong process and that the consumer is one drug/drink away from relapse and continuing from whence one left off. And there are those who think that the illness mutates into some other form of obsessive-compulsive behavior, like gambling, religion, work, relationship, etc. So, the term cured is as ambiguous as the illness itself. I use the term manageable because just like any other chronic disease, one can go in and out of remission. They have to maintain the medical protocol that works for them and constantly monitor their condition.

At what point does substance use become dependence?

Substance use dependence is as varied and unique as the persons who suffers with the disease. Because of the insidiousness of the disease, it is difficult to pinpoint the subtle transition from use to abuse to dependence. For example, a person's drug of choice can defer from their drug of dependence and they may not know it. I used most psychoactive substances and became abusive of them all: heroin, cocaine, cannabis, benzodiazepines, alcohol, etc., but my substance of dependence was alcohol, and it happened with my first drink. I later learned that you never get higher than your first experience, all attempts after that are trying to obtain that first experience again.

Imagine the first time you ate ice cream, your favorite flavor, or any experience that brought you satisfaction or euphoria. Each and every one of us are seeking ways and means to feel good about ourselves. No one ever thinks that what appears to make them happy can eventually become the catalyst that will create so much sadness and pain in their lives and the lives of their family and friends.

Our focus in treating substance use disorder is psychoeducation on a spiritual, mental and emotional level. If the illness is at the point where it has caused sociological (family, housing, food) and neurological (nerves) deficiency, then treatment must be intensified to address such needs. It is extremely important that the treatment protocol is comprehensive and culturally sensitive. And the attitude of the treatment team must always be positive and optimistic.

I remember a story of a man falling from a ten-story building and he lived. When the paramedics approached him and looked at his condition, they were looking at him as if he were a lost cause. As one of the medics was doing his usual questioning, everyone else was looking on just knowing that the man wasn't going to make it. Now, the man seeing this pessimism knew that he had to come up with something to change their attitudes to save his own life. So, when the medic asked if he was allergic to anything? The man said, "Yes. I'm allergic to gravity and height!" Everybody started laughing and it changed their approach to helping him. According to the story, the man is alive and well.

The negative stigma of substance use disorder and its

pathologies chronically affects the outcome of treatment protocols. So much so that research for the last thirty years has determined that only 30% of any treatment population will have positive outcomes and go on to long term sustained remission. Even though many of our medical protocols from other diseases have a lesser rate of positive outcome, we can do better. Attitude, empathy, teamwork across disciplines, and putting the consumer first—and not necessarily in this order—is H.O.W. (Honesty, Open-mindedness & Willingness) it works. No big I's and little u's! As a professional practitioner in long term recovery, this H.O.W. model is the best I've seen in my thirty plus years in the field.

What is Post Incarceration Syndrome (PICS)? How does it relate to Post Traumatic Stress Disorder (PTSD)?

One of the most prolific scholars in relapse prevention, Terence T. Gorski, introduced a diagnosis Post Incarceration Syndrome (PICS) which is a serious problem that contributes to relapse in the addicted and mentally ill offenders once they are released from correctional institutions. It has been suggested that released prisoners experience a unique set of mental health symptoms related to, but not limited to, Post-Traumatic Stress Disorder (PTSD). Research proves that there is a recognizable Post Incarceration Syndrome that comes from the unique effects of incarceration on mental health.

There was a study conducted with 25 released "lifers" (individuals serving a life sentence), who served an average of 19 years in a state correctional institution. The researchers assessed to what extent the symptoms described by the participants overlapped with other mental disorders, most notably Post Traumatic Stress Disorder. The narratives indicate a specific cluster of mental health symptoms. In addition to PTSD, this cluster was characterized by institutionalized personality traits, social–sensory disorientation, and alienation. In light of this, I would suggest that Post Incarceration Syndrome constitutes a discrete subtype of PTSD that results from long-term imprisonment. Recognizing Post Incarceration Syndrome may allow for more adequate recognition of the effects of incarceration and treatment among ex-inmates and ultimately, successful re-entry into society.

The most prevalent features of chronic PTSD reported by the interviewees were recurrent distressing dreams; hyper arousal (sleep disturbances), isolation and problems with intimate relationships. Recurrent distressing dreams mostly involved the prison experience, "When I got out, I was tormented by nightmares that I was still in prison. I'd wake up sittin' and screamin'. Cold sweat pouring down my face, literally, and my pillow soaked [...] They were all prison nightmares and some of them were me... seeing myself waking up in prison [...] Those were really bad, when I [first] got out, they were almost debilitating." [Male, age 53]

Additionally, signs of hyper arousal included startled responses, at times accumulating into full-blown panic attacks. "Like, you know I take the ride here, and if I get into crowds or I'm in open spaces or things like that... It brings on panic attacks. And the panic attacks bring on seizures. But, cause to me, it's like I can't go outside, and walk around the compound because I'm in wide open spaces and there's nothing around me, to like, to hold onto if I start feeling panicky [...]. [Male, age 64]

The inability to engage in relationships was also reflected in intimate relations. "[In prison] you have to distance yourself, so you always have to keep on putting up walls, and putting up barriers, every single day. You have to build like this shell around you, to protect you from your environment. So, if you keep on doing this for so long, then once you get let out, it's kind of difficult to bring it down, because it's ingrained in you. [S]o, one of the things she [my girlfriend] has a problem with, is like [...] you're unemotional. And I tell her, I'm like, listen I'm defective right now, I'm messed up right now. [Male, age 37]

The generational effect of PICS/PTSD in families is

similar to the generational effect of substance use disorder. There are some definitive factors known as genetic and environmental predisposition. The mystery of the illness, however, is which family member will become directly affected by the illness. There is also the indirect effect wherein a family member may overcompensate mentally, physically and socially to evade and/or avoid what they see happening in the family. This person usually becomes very successful but tends to lack in social interactions and intimate relationships. Many of them find themselves in the helping professions of behavioral/mental healthcare, substance use or criminal justice. And last but not least on this point, we must understand that any mental health or substance use disorder is a family illness meaning that the family reacts on an emotional level as does the family member with the diagnosis. Therefore, treatment must include the entire family for the most effective outcome.

It is crucial for the mental/behavioral care and substance use clinician, psychologist, psychiatrist, social worker, etc., to understand the relationship between Post Incarceration Syndrome and Post-Traumatic Stress Disorder when working with returning citizens (prisoner re-entry). Most healthcare professionals, politicians, etc., think that giving a returning citizen a job is sufficient; this is no more correct than it would be for a person returning home from the war in Iraq or Vietnam. The treatment approach in these cases must be empathic, genuine and reality based. The time limit with these individuals are as varied as the persons and the experiences that were precursors to the period of incarceration. NO HUMAN BEING WAS CREATED TO BE IN A CAGE! The psychological effect on a person imprisoned is devastating. The very steel that is used to make the prisons is designed to drain the human being of his/her natural energy. The thought of being deprived of your natural freedom, proper nutrition and normal intimate relationships is devastating and produces deep-seated psychosis over time.

Therapy for this population is a must, and it must be administered with the same regard as any other mental/behavioral health diagnosis if the person is to be given a full chance for recovery. No soldier returns from battle without being debriefed and re-socialized and provided with the necessary support to return to normal citizenship. It should be the same for the returning incarcerated. He/she has survived a battle that is not normal to human comprehension. In fact, Gorski learned through further research that most victims of incarceration who are best able to endure such an experience are those who are rooted in a profound religious and/or spiritual connection. Such persons seem to have been able to transform their physical reality into livable condition. However, when they come home, if they do not continue their religious practices in earnest, recidivism is almost instantaneous.

Medical Marijuana

The subject of medical marijuana for me is a very interesting phenomenon. In my twenty plus years of psychoactive substance use in the 1960s and early 1970s, with marijuana being one of the primary substances of choice for me, I remember some of my closest friends referring to it as medicine. What did they know that the world had yet to learn? My mentor, chief consultant and spirit guide, Professor Albert Dickens, the author of *Uncle Yah Yah 21st Century Man of Wisdom*, foretold the legalization of marijuana at least thirty years ago. So, I researched what is written in this section for the reader to catch up to where I am as it relates to treatment, medication assisted treatment, and evidenced-based or better yet proven practice. When we talk about being eclectic in our approach to treatment, we have to remember HOW recovery works, Honesty Open mindedness Willingness!

More than half of the U.S. and the District of Columbia have legalized medical marijuana in some form, and more are considering bills to do the same. Yet while many people are using marijuana, the Food and Drug Administration (FDA) has only approved it for treatment of two rare and severe forms of epilepsy, Dravet syndrome and Lennox-Gastaut syndrome.

Why hasn't more research been done? One reason is that the U.S. Drug Enforcement Administration (DEA) considers marijuana a Schedule I drug; the same as heroin, LSD, and ecstasy. They consider that marijuana is likely to be abused and lacks in medical value. "Because of that, researchers need a special license to study it," says Marcel Bonn-Miller, PhD, a substance abuse specialist at the University of Pennsylvania Perelman School of Medicine.

That may not change anytime soon. The DEA considered reclassifying marijuana as a Schedule II drug like Ritalin or oxycodone, but decided to keep it as a Schedule I drug.

The agency did, however, agree to support additional research on marijuana and make the process easier for researchers. "Research is critically needed, because we have to be able to advise patients and doctors on the safe and effective use of cannabis," Bonn-Miller says.

He shared some background on medical marijuana's uses and potential side effects.

What is medical marijuana?

Medical marijuana is made of dried parts of the *Cannabis sativa* plant. Humans have turned to it as an herbal remedy for centuries, and today people use it to relieve symptoms or treat various diseases. The Federal Government still considers it illegal, but some states allow it to treat specific health problems. The FDA, the U.S. agency that regulates medicines, hasn't approved the plant as a treatment for any conditions.

Medical marijuana uses the marijuana plant or chemicals in it to treat diseases or conditions. It's basically the same product as recreational marijuana, but it's taken for medical purposes.

The marijuana plant contains more than 100 different chemicals called cannabinoids. Each one has a different effect on the body. Delta-9-tetrahydrocannabinol (THC) and cannabidiol (CBD) are the main chemicals used in medicine. THC also produces the "high" people feel when they smoke marijuana or eat foods containing it.

What is medical marijuana used for?

More and more states are legalizing marijuana to treat pain and illness. Medical marijuana is used to treat a number of different conditions, including

- Alzheimer's disease
- Appetite loss
- Cancer
- Crohn's disease

- Eating disorders such as anorexia
- Epilepsy
- Glaucoma
- Mental health conditions like schizophrenia and posttraumatic stress disorder (PTSD)
- Multiple sclerosis
- Muscle spasms
- Nausea
- Pain
- Wasting syndrome (cachexia)

"But it's not yet proven to help many of these conditions, with a few exceptions. The greatest amount of evidence for the therapeutic effects of cannabis relate to its ability to reduce chronic pain, nausea and vomiting due to chemotherapy, and spasticity (tight or stiff muscles) from MS," Bonn-Miller says.

How does it help?

Cannabinoids, the active chemicals in medical marijuana, are similar to chemicals the body makes that are involved in appetite, memory, movement, and pain.

Research suggests cannabinoids might:

- Reduce anxiety

- Reduce inflammation and relieve pain
- Control nausea and vomiting caused by cancer chemotherapy
- Kill cancer cells and slow tumor growth
- Relax tight muscles in people with MS
- Stimulate appetite and improve weight gain in people with cancer and AIDS

How can medical marijuana help with seizure disorders?

Medical marijuana received a lot of attention a few years ago when parents said that a special form of the drug helped control seizures in their children. The FDA recently approved Epidiolex, which is made from CBD, as a therapy for people with very severe or hard-to-treat seizures. In studies, some people had a dramatic drop in seizures after taking this drug.

Which states allow medical marijuana?

Medical marijuana is legal in these 33 states and the District of Columbia.

- Alaska
- Arizona
- Arkansas
- California
- Colorado

- Connecticut
- Delaware
- District of Columbia
- Florida
- Hawaii
- Illinois
- Louisiana
- Maine
- Maryland
- Massachusetts
- Michigan
- Minnesota
- Missouri
- Montana
- Nevada
- New Hampshire
- New Jersey
- New Mexico
- New York
- North Dakota
- Ohio
- Oklahoma
- Oregon
- Pennsylvania
- Rhode Island

- Utah
- Vermont
- Washington
- West Virginia

States that allow restricted use only include Alabama, Georgia, Iowa, Kentucky, Mississippi, Missouri, North Carolina, South Carolina, Virginia, Wisconsin and Wyoming.

How do you get medical marijuana?

To get medical marijuana, you need a written recommendation from a licensed doctor in states where it is legal (not every doctor is willing to recommend medical marijuana for their patients.). You must have a condition that qualifies for medical marijuana use. Each state has its own list of qualifying conditions. Your state may also require you to get a medical marijuana ID card. Once you have that card, you can buy medical marijuana at a store called a dispensary.

How do you take it?

To take medical marijuana, you can:

- Smoke it
- Inhale it through a device called a vaporizer that turns it into a mist

- Eat it -- for example, in a brownie or lollipop
- Apply it to your skin in a lotion, spray, oil, or cream
- Place a few drops of the liquid form under your tongue

How you take it is up to you. Each method works differently in your body. "If you smoke or vaporize cannabis, you feel the effects very quickly," Bonn-Miller says. "If you eat it, it takes significantly longer. It can take 1 to 2 hours to experience the effects from edible products."

Has the FDA approved medical marijuana?

The FDA has approved two man-made cannabinoid medicines -- dronabinol (Marinol, Syndros) and nabilone (Cesamet) -- to treat nausea and vomiting from chemotherapy. The cannabidiol Epidiolex was approved in 2018 for treating seizures associated with two rare and severe forms of epilepsy, Lennox-Gastaut syndrome and Dravet syndrome.

What are the side effects of medical marijuana?

Side effects that have been reported include:

- Bloodshot eyes

- Depression
- Dizziness
- Fast heartbeat
- Hallucinations
- Low blood pressure

The drug can also affect judgment and coordination, which could lead to accidents and injuries. When used during the teenage years, when the brain is still developing, marijuana might affect IQ and mental function.

Slideshow: Medical Marijuana

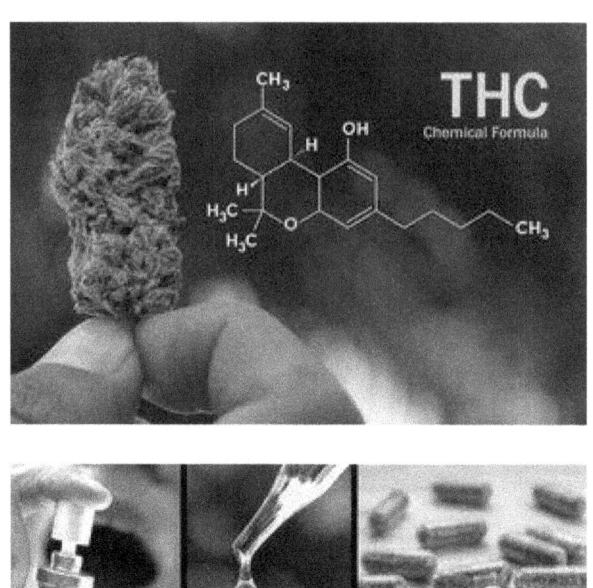

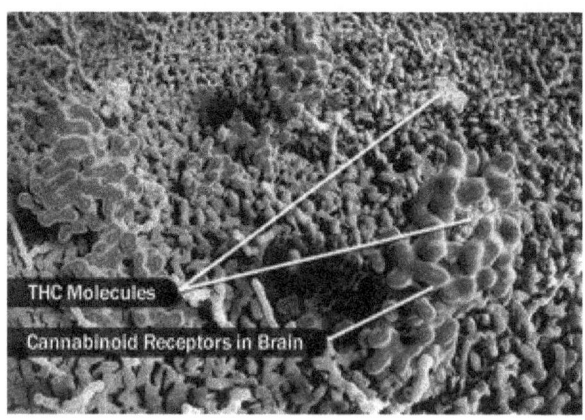

How It Works in Your Body

The chemicals in marijuana affect you when they connect with specific parts of cells called receptors. Scientists know that you have cells with cannabinoid receptors in your brain and in your immune system. But the exact process of how the drug affects them isn't clear yet.

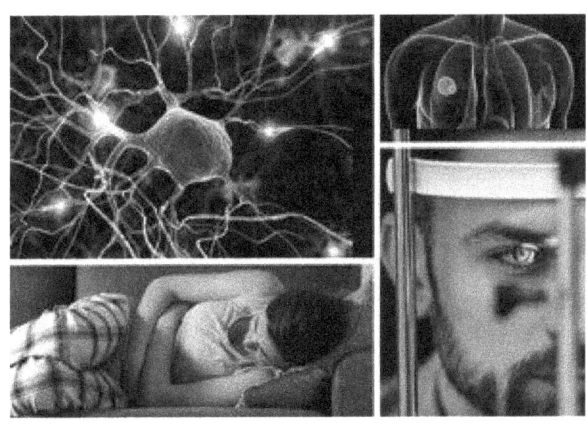

Are There Risks?

Because marijuana contains some of the same

chemicals found in tobacco, there have been concerns that smoking it could harm the lungs. The effects of inhaled marijuana on lung health aren't clear, but there's some evidence that it might increase the risk for bronchitis and other lung problems.

If you smoke it, you could have breathing problems such as chronic cough and bronchitis. Research has linked cannabis use and car accidents. If you use it while pregnant, you may affect your baby's health and development. Studies also show a tie between pot and psychotic disorders such as schizophrenia.

Another issue is that the FDA doesn't oversee medical marijuana like it does prescription drugs. Although states monitor and regulate sales, they often don't have the resources to do so. That means the strength of and ingredients in medical marijuana can differ quite a bit depending on where you buy it. "We did a study last year in which we purchased labeled edible products, like brownies and lollipops, in California and Washington. Then we sent them to the lab," Bonn-Miller says. "Few of the products contained anywhere near what they said they did. That's a problem."

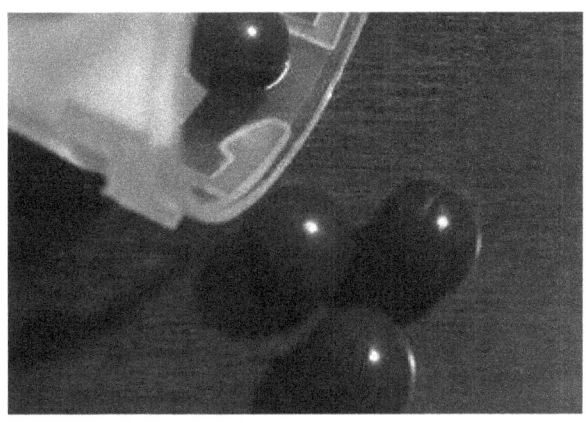

What Are FDA-Approved Versions of Medical Marijuana?

Although the Federal Government hasn't given its OK to marijuana for medicinal use, it has signed off on three related compounds as specific treatments. If you have nausea caused by chemotherapy, you might take a synthetic cannabinoid, either dronabinol or nabilone. Dronabinol also can help boost the appetite for people with AIDS. The FDA approved cannabidiol (Epidiolex) as a treatment for two rare kinds of epilepsy.

Are There Any Laws in Conflict Regarding Medical Marijuana?

California was the first state to legalize medical marijuana, in 1996. Since then, more than half the states in the U.S. have done so (recreational weed is also legal in some places.). But the Federal Government still considers it an illegal drug, which can create confusion. For instance, even if you have a prescription, the Transportation Security Administration doesn't allow cannabis in your luggage.

Do People Become Addicted?

The National Institute on Drug Abuse says marijuana can be addictive and is considered a "gateway drug" to using other drugs. "The higher the level of THC and the more often you use, the more likely you are to become dependent," Bonn-Miller says. "You have difficulty stopping if you need to stop. You have cravings during periods when you're not using. And you need more and more of it to have the same effect."

Doctors don't know much about the addiction risk for people who use the drug for medical reasons, and it needs more study. But people who use marijuana to get high can go on to have substance misuse issues. The most common problem is dependence. If you're dependent, you'll feel withdrawal symptoms if you stop using. If you're addicted—a more severe problem—you're unable to go without the drug.

Extracting THC from Marijuana

Why Don't We Know More?

Although cannabis has been an herbal remedy for centuries, the evidence for how well it works is lacking in many cases. Scientists prefer large studies with certain types of controls before they draw conclusions, and much of the research thus far hasn't met those standards. Products vary in strength and it's hard to measure doses, which has made judging the benefits of marijuana even more complicated.

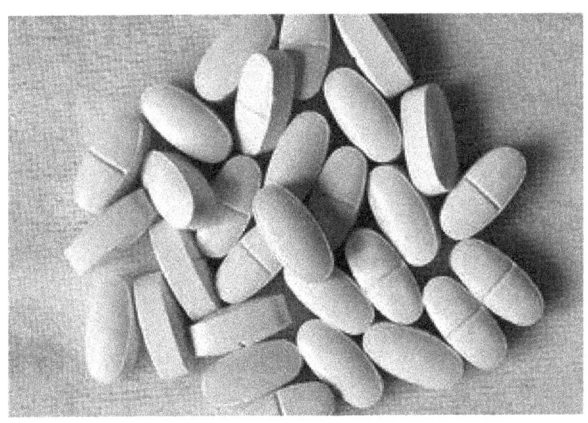

Is Cannabis an Opioid Alternative?

Could cannabis help solve issues involving these powerful painkillers? In some states with legal weed, prescriptions for this pain medicine fell and researchers found a link to fewer overdose deaths. But another study found a link between pot use and abuse of these narcotic drugs. Scientists need more evidence before they can say for sure.

References

Article: How Medical Marijuana Works, and Which Conditions It Treats

SOURCES:
For FAQ

Marcel Bonn-Miller, PhD, adjunct assistant professor, University of Pennsylvania Perelman School of Medicine.

National Conference of State Legislatures: "State Medical Marijuana Laws."

National Institute on Drug Abuse: "Drug Facts: Is Marijuana Medicine?" "Is Marijuana Addictive?"

Drug Enforcement Administration: "Drug Schedules."

Department of Health and Human Services.

Kaur, R. *Current Clinical Pharmacology*, April 2016.

PDQ Integrative, Alternative, and Complementary Therapies Editorial Board: "Cannabis and Cannabinoids (PDQ)."

Schrot, R. *Annals of Medicine*, May 2016.

Epilepsy Foundation: "Learn About Medical Marijuana and Epilepsy."

News release, Ohio Gov. John Kasich's office.

News release, Insys Therapeutics, Inc.

For Marijuana Map:

WebMD Article Reviewed by Neil Lava, MD on December 15, 2018

Governing.com: "State Marijuana Laws Map."

NCSL: "State Medical Marijuana Laws."

www.ingramcontent.com/pod-product-compliance
Lightning Source LLC
Chambersburg PA
CBHW041319110526
44591CB00021B/2837